Collected Poems of Edmund Skellings

Collected Poems
1958–1998

Edmund Skellings
Poet Laureate of Florida

University Press of Florida
Gainesville Tallahassee Tampa Boca Raton
Pensacola Orlando Miami Jacksonville

Copyright 1960, 1961, 1976, 1977, 1978, 1985, 1998 by Edmund Skellings
Printed in the United States of America on acid-free paper
All rights reserved

03 02 01 00 99 98   6 5 4 3 2 1

The foreword, by Donald Kaufman, is reprinted from the *Massachusetts Review,* copyright 1979, The Massachusetts Review, Inc., by permission.

Library of Congress Cataloging-in-Publication Data

Skellings, Edmund.
[Poems]
Collected poems, 1958–1998 / Edmund Skellings.
p. cm.
ISBN 0-8130-1606-1 (alk. paper)
I. Title.
PS3537.K33A17 1998   98-19847
811'.54—dc21

The University Press of Florida is the scholarly publishing agency for the State University System of Florida, comprising Florida A & M University, Florida Atlantic University, Florida International University, Florida State University, University of Central Florida, University of Florida, University of North Florida, University of South Florida, and University of West Florida.

University Press of Florida
15 Northwest 15th Street
Gainesville, FL 32611
http://nersp.nerdc.ufl.edu/~upf

To my dear wife,
Louise Noah Skellings,
who helped me with
all these poems

Contents

Foreword xv
Acknowledgments xxviii

HEART ATTACKS (1976)
Frost to Skellings, 3
Incantation 4
At Sunland Training Center 5
To His Machine 6
Crown 7
The Double Helix 8
Fictions Personal 11
Prices 12
Up North 13
Yerkish 14
He Says She Says 15
Oval 16
Social Security 17
Conventions 18
Treasures 19
Hemingway 20
The Leningrad Writers Conference 1942 21
Memory 22
Remembering Mailer 23
Another Oval 25
An Archeological Site in France 26
Extrapolation 29
Naturalist 30
Science Fiction 32
Epilog 34
From the Striped Chair 35
Amulet 37
Surface Tensions 38
Grizzly 39
Tout 40
The Elbow Room 41
Home Made Candy 42
Shooting Match 43

The Hartford Circus Fire 44
Warning 48
Even America 49
On the Patio 50
The Tanks of Amherst 51
The Collected Me 52
A Bare Walk 53
Movements 54
Cavendish 56
Monday at the Airport 57
Series 59
Hand Calculator 60
On Instruments 61

FACE VALUE (1977)

Opening Shock 65
Dass Ich Erkenne 66
Tectonic 67
Extra Extra 68
Bicentennial History Lesson 69
1976 Florida Almanac 71
Alaska 73
On the Death of Your Father 74
Male Lead 76
Radio John 77
Timer 78
Vitamin 79
Three Around the Young Gentleman
   Way Out on the Way Out 80
   Ends 81
   On Falling 82
What's Mine 83
For a Friend with Two Years to Live 84
Heartwood 85
Leavings 87
Shorelines 88
Folklore 89
The Dystrophy of Certain Muscles 90
Friendly Game 91
Monarch 92
Fairbanks, Alaska 93

Louise Is from Iowa   94
So Lonely in Hartford   95
Children's Verse   96
Librarian   97
Artistic   98
Only Eyes   99
Specialty   100
Advertising   101
Likeness   102
Flying Circus   103
A Dark Outline   104
Pro Vita Sua   105
A Needle's Eye   106
Central System   107
To a Beauty   108
Resort   109
Tongues   110
Creative Writing Notebook: Lesson No.1   111
Melodramatics   112
The Prom: Three Poems
   The Queen   114
   Wallflower   115
   Chaperone   116
Moon Poems
   Projection   117
   The Tracks of Tyros   118
   Moon Flight   120
Blues in Black and White
   Down in the Ghetto   122
   Welfare Shout   123
   Sharpy   124
   Owner   124
   Understanding Is a Tone of Voice Blues   125
   Understanding Is a Tone of Voice Blues Part Two   126
   How to Pick a Mistress, Or   127
A Writer's Attic   128

SHOWING MY AGE (1978)

Eddie's Bar   131
Pruning Roots   132
Black and White and Color   133

Torsion 134
Cartwheels 135
Foils 136
Over the Gulf 137
Talk 138
Organization of American States 139
Spider 140
Inside Knowledge 141
Jack Smith, Magician 142
Forty Four 143
Runner 144
Peripatetic 145
Doctor of Medicine 146
Storages 150
Florida versus Zamora 151
The Final Days 153
Calendar 155
The Inner Ear 156
Atop the Ford Foundation 158
Here Today 159
South Beach When 160
Federated Stores 161
Salutations 162
Metaphysical 163
Forty 164
Bed Time Story 165
The Dania Pier 166
While the Moon Is Listening 167
The Ghost of Polonius 168
Moonflight II 169
Extra Vehicular Activity 170
The Day after the New Year 171
Blackbeard 172
Bulldozer 173
Last Man on the Moon 174
Einstein at the Cafe Bulwark 176
Travelers Inn 177
Caesar Poet 178
Magic 179
Touring in the Mountains 180
In Florida 181

Diagnoses   182
Garbage Can Blues   183
The Poet as a Contemporary Reflection   184
The Dream Ants   185
Abstraction Blooded   186
Showing My Age (21 Genes)   187

LIVING PROOF (1985)

Ocean   199
Opening Poem   200
Vincent, Vincent   201
Paul Gauguin   202
Ages   203
Black Hole   204
Robert Frost   205
Chicopee River   206
Prayer   207
Artificial Intelligence   208
Words for Jesus of Nazareth   209
Florida   211
Tutankhamen Traveling   212
Gulliver   213
Poem for Wyatt Wyatt   214
Janice   215
Morning   216
Florida Turnpike   217
Memo of Compliance   218
Key Largo   220
Time Study   221
Her Class Reunion   222
The Bells   223
Courses   224
Eye Teeth   225
Statuesque   226
Vocals   227
Free Climbing   228
Clear Moon   229
Notes on Relative Inertia   230
News Brief   231
Driver Ed   232
Nuclear   233

Gladiatorial 234
Senior Citizen 235
Carnival 236
Love Song in Age 237
Down Home Question 238
Down Home Answer 239
Music 240
Choochoo Train 241
Loving Memory 242
Comic Poem 243
Sleight Of 244

PERSONAL EFFECTS (1998)

Ada 247
Miami Heart 248
Tosa Mitsusada 250
Dry Tears 251
Reader 252
Country Poem 253
Art in Heaven 254
Whiteout 255
Cat Sonnet 256
Occupational Hazards 257
Melville 258
Long Distance 259
Salt Seas 260
Eucharist 261
Two Sides 262
Two en Route 263
Two from Home 264
Business Plan 265
To Walk Thin Ice 266
Cruises 267
Choice 268
Shakespeare 269
Knockout 270
Old Twist 271
Exercise #1 272
Playthings in the Playhouse 273
The Laureate Game 275
Alaska Tandem 276

Remembering My Liberal Education 277
Regret Park 278
Cultures 279
The Poem in America 280
Fruits 281
In Age 282
Late Night 283
Ideally 284
Giverny 285
Duet 286
Remembrances of Things Past 287
St. Paul's Church 288
Dedication 289
White on White 290
Aft to Bridge 291
Epilogue 292

Foreword

Skellings' *Nearing the Milennium*:
Heart Attacks, Face Value, Showing My Age

Donald L. Kaufmann

Like Walt Whitman, Edmund Skellings is one of America's Orphic poets. The main thread that binds Skellings' trilogy, *Nearing the Millennium*, together echoes Whitman's attempt to humanize the discoveries and inventions of scientists and engineers. So does the British writer, C. P. Snow, in more recent times. With his concept of the Two Cultures, which peaked in visibility in the early 1960's, Snow sees the millennium nearing the darker tones of Yeats in "The Second Coming." This arrival of an intellectual darkness stems from Snow's belief in the split that has continued to widen between the world of science and technology and the world of humanities and the arts. In each Culture, overspecialization has resulted in a compartmentalization which has made communication impossible and has set the arts and sciences at war with each other. Surveying the prevailing spirit and the ends and means of current American poetry reveals little or no awareness of the continual distrust and alienation between the Two Cultures. A little over a century ago, Whitman foresaw the need to combine the ends and means of science and art.

> Singing my days,
> Singing the great achievements of the present,
> Singing the strong, light works of engineers,
> Our modern wonders, . . .

. . . So begins Whitman's "Passage to India," written in 1871. Whitman celebrates three recent epoch-making events: the opening of the Suez Canal; the spanning of the North American continent by railroad; the completion of the Atlantic cable. In all three, Whitman sees the possibility of the coming of an age of universal peace and brotherhood. Since Whitman, American poets have tended either to ignore the workings of science and technology or to see them as pure evils. Thus, American poetry has blinded itself to any open evaluation or understanding of the industrial revolution and has locked itself within what C. P. Snow calls "the transitional culture (which) responds by wishing the future did not exist." But such cultural myopia is absent from Edmund Skellings' *An American Poetry Trilogy.* That is the chief reason why reading *Nearing the Millennium* is such a refreshing experience. American poetry, for once, is eyeballing Lord Snow's Two Cultures.

As the title of Skellings' trilogy indicates, the winding down toward A.D. 2000 marks the end of an age of high technology and, probably, the zenith of America's power to be the world's tastemaker. The way presentday America consumes the products of science and technology is the way of the world. Today's Whitman, therefore, can find no ready-made optimism. Technological man, with America as prototype, is running out of time. Natural resources are being squandered. Personhood is going. There is a sense of a Doomed America (a Doomed World?) that permeates Skellings' trilogy. But Skellings does not barrage his readers with poems overtly from the viewpoint of the environmentalist and existentialist. Skellings, instead, opens both himself and his verse to the wonders (or horrors?) of the sciences. This results in the most sustained use of science poetry in recent times.

Dante was probably the last poet to know all the sciences of his day, and probably not since Donne and Shelley have there been any good poets of science, even including Whitman, who welcomed the glories of the sciences without much understanding of them. Of course, with today's proliferation of knowledge and specialization in all areas of science, no one poet can be expected to be another Dante. But Skellings adopts the next best strategy. He does not rely on that kind of science poetry which is discursive and informational, meant both to educate and entertain. The more authentic science poetry is what Skellings creates. His aim is not to explain, but to discover. In this kind of science poetry, the poet himself can simulate the ways of the scientist not afraid to speculate and discover beyond the normal confines of his discipline. For example, the poem "Specialty" begins: "Glottochronology is my favorite / Science, though you'd never heard / About it . . ." That is true. "Glottochronology" is Skellings' own fake science. Such fakery also extends to the creatures in "Naturalist." Here the reader is introduced to such phenoms as the "Yellow Spinesnake" and "Andrew's Lacewing / A very intelligent bird. . ." Naturally, the sound and tone here is part fun and play (Skellings' verse is seldom shy of humor). But such fakery of the spirit of science also has overtones that are both philosophic and esthetic. If a poet like Skellings can make light sport of science while deifying it, then the reader may grow aware of the similarities (not the differences) between science and art. Both thrive on a sense of wonder and a desire for elegance, and both rely on inspiration to carry them to the ultimate experience with mystery. And both science and art insist on a certain methodology, especially the principles of selection, inclusion and concentration. Such structural principles are the essence of science poetry, since it reflects both disciplines, and this is the basis upon which Skellings designs and constructs his trilogy. *Nearing the Millennium* runs on order and method. It is rooted in architecture, and the word "architecture" itself is both a science and an art.

Each of the books in Skellings' trilogy has its own theme cluster. Man and Nature sets up the bulk of poems in the first volume, *Heart Attacks*. Here, images of animals, plants and other natural phenomena abound so as to reveal the biological limits (both inner and outer) of life. Volume Two, *Face Value*, shifts to the theme of Man and Man. Here, with a collection of individual portraits, Skellings concentrates on the value of the person. But again, there is a preoccupation with limitations. Most of these human portraits focus on genetic defects, and the many references to the bodies (especially the face and tongue) of these cripples all point to the genetic limits to our physical shape. Again, Skellings is as much the scientist as the poet. *Showing My Age* investigates the tension of Man and Society. Toward the middle of this third and final volume, Skellings dissects (the wit softening the satire) various power areas of American Society, administrators and politicians in "The Ghost of Polonius" and the judiciary system in "Florida vs Zamora" and so on. But Skellings begins this book with a few personal poems about his own age and youth, before extending his vision to include the human family, and then concludes the volume with the brilliant title poem, "Showing My Age," which is broken into "21 Genes." With this strategy of evolving from the personal to the universal, self and society are merged and, in the process, Skellings not only "shows" his own "age" but his culture's "age" as well.

For a fuller understanding of Skellings' American trilogy, a reader should (ideally) have a layman's knowledge of the current climate in the natural and social sciences. Skellings certainly does. Everywhere in *Nearing the Millennium* there are signs that Skellings' poetry belongs to the post-Einstein universe of subatomic physics where all rules of existence fall apart. Like the anachronistic Polonius, the ghosts of Plato and Newton with their fixed forms have been put to rest. Now Skellings, like the physicists, ponders a new order of reality based on non-Euclidean geometry which conceives of space not as straight but curved. As long as the sub-atomic physicists cannot predict the location of the electron, then the essential stuff of nature is but a packet of energy in flux and that includes such icons in human existence once thought to be fixtures, and therefore recognizable, such as Love, Soul and Life itself. All there is is mass changing the nature of space. Existence has no cause and effects, no ends or means or beginnings. "I can't believe that God plays dice with the universe," said Einstein, an orthodox Jew, who spent the rest of his life trying to disprove what he had already proved. But Skellings, seeking questions rather than answers, lets the spirit of his poetry be as aleatory as God's supposed dice. The uncertain outcome of human existence (including the creation of verse) means that the locus of the mystery (since Dante, Milton and Whitman) has changed. Its roots are now in the sciences. For Skellings, the most religious and awesome function of the poet is to discover the face of God in physics and biology.

The mystery of human intelligence, its nature and evolution and esthetic values, is what lies at the heart of *Nearing the Millennium*. In the more philosophical poems, "The Double Helix," "On Instruments," "Dass Ich Erkenne," "Showing My Age," Skellings attempts to discover an identity between Reimannian (or non-Euclidian) geometry and the structure and shape of the DNA and the corpus callosum of the brain. Skellings also often alludes to the current lab probes into the "split brain." This hypothesis conceives of the brain as functioning in hemispheres, the left hemisphere activity involved in complex functioning and the control of speech, while the right hemisphere is adapted for the manipulation of spatial relationships and the perception of non-verbal material. Certain neuropsychologists believe that the new frontier in human intelligence will be the gradual and eventual consolidation of hemispheric functions and that will signal the next step in the evolution of man. This possibility of a superior human endowed with the skills of a mental ambidextrian intrigues Skellings and brightens his vision and keeps his verse from slipping into doomsday sounds of God's clicking dice in an aleatory universe. Such nihilism seems inconceivable, especially when science and poetry join in an attempt to discover a new perception of man. Current voices of science are everywhere in Skellings' trilogy. There are echoes in Carl Sagan's *The Dragons of Eden: Speculations on the Evolution of Human Intelligence*, and *Clinical Neuropsychology* by Edgar Miller and *The Tao of Physics* by Fritjof Capra. What results is poetry that reflects on quantum theory, on Heisenberg's "Principle of Uncertainty," and on the dialectics of human intelligence and other mysteries. Lord Snow should be pleased with the one staple in Skellings' trilogy, that the Two Cultures here are at eye level.

Skellings also attempts to harmonize the voices of science and poetry. Throughout *Nearing the Millennium,* the diction is pitched at the middle, a tasty blend of high science and layman idiom. Language is on a mission here. There is a conscious attempt to break down snobbery between scientist and artist. Formal scientific terms are used sparingly. Jargon and other incommunicables are avoided. Skellings also makes no use of the stratospheric words of academic poetry. The language of the trilogy, instead, runs on one principle, making the complex as simple as possible. There is enough uncertainty in the way scientists look at the universe without the language of poetry contributing. But there are times when Skellings pushes layman idiom to the extremes of jivey flippancy. Such a recourse to irreverent slang is probably Skellings' way of disturbing those artists and humanists who are smug over their formalities of opposition to science and technology.

All these stratagems of language must conform to the architectural principle of Skellings' mode of science poetry, where, like art and science, content and method must mirror each other. For example, in the poem "Extrapolation":

> Most of us is math, which comes as no
> Surprise: The limbs of trees circle
> The trunk, leaves the branch, all
> Spin slowly the great tap root. This
> Can be seen from palm frond about
> The nut, arms and legs popping from
> The spine, twinned brains blooming.
> Go down deep and you hit math. Every
> Time. Darwin shaped it up by
> Statistics. A natural arithmetic.
> He stopped there, but because each
> Poem should have one great idea,
> Here: Extrapolation is genetic.
> That should account for you, big eyes.

Here John Donne has gone into reverse. The 17th-century metaphysical poet would first allude to his lady fair and / or coy mistress before "extrapolating" the nature of his love by the use of conceits based on then current sciences. Today's counterpart of the metaphysical poet, like Skellings, must contend with the possibility that science is as great a mystery as is love. That is what the architecture of "Extrapolation" seems to be saying. "Extrapolation" begins and ends with content and technique reflecting each other. Perhaps Skellings' forte as a poetic stylist is his careful practice of enjambment. Instead of the predictability of end-stops, Skellings prefers to break off in the interior of the sentence. Breaking off at the wrong places? Not for a modern metaphysician like Skellings. Meaning becomes multiple at the point of enjambment in "Extrapolation" and elsewhere. Such a studied use of enjambment also creates a mood of dismemberment within the poetry that reflects the piecemeal universe of curved space and slippery neutrons. Heisenberg has his "Principle of Uncertainty" and Skellings has his enjambment which becomes the vehicle of "a natural arithmetic."

"Extrapolation" also demonstrates other salient traits of the modern metaphysical poem. On the quest for profundity, the diction remains simple. The persona tries to balance the esthetic with the scientific. Symmetry can be beautiful. Metrical and rhythmic schemes of each 7-line stanza reflect each other. Rhyme would be more appropriate in a Newtonian universe. Sound and sense also unite in the prevailing image of the cyclic tree being linked to the "twinned brains blooming" of the Double Helix. Today's genetic engineer and science-poet would agree that to compare the "great tap root" with the DNA is no longer an outlandish yoking or what John Donne would have called a "conceit." Today's science-poet must seek moderation between the Two Cultures. To assure such an accommodation, the persona must keep to a balanced tone. His attitude toward science must be respectful without sounding pompous, while, at the same time, he must grant equal time to the esthetic man within. Humor is the best tonal catalyst. Wit is a trademark of a Skellings poem. By making the dialogue between the Two Cultures humorous, Skellings also makes such mysteries as human intelligence and love understandably human. So a poet can pontificate his "one great idea" with consolation, "Extrapolation is genetic," as long as he does not neglect the lady of his life, "That should account for you, big eyes." Dante's Beatrice? Laura of Petrarch's sonnets? Donne would begin his metaphysical poem with his lady fair and Skellings ends his with his "big eyes." Human, witty, even a whiff of romance, but still, the real mystery lady of "Extrapolation" seems to be Science.

From the current riches of biology, physics, mathematics, chemistry, astronomy and archeology, Skellings sees the shaping forces of human experience emanating from the curves of the chromosome. Or, as expressed in the concluding lines of the long poem "The Double Helix":

And the helix twists of infinity
And time is the turn of the twist

And the spine stems and the fingers leaf
And the eyes flower

Oh saddle shaped light
Oh inky rider

Earlier in the poem, Skellings has alerted his reader to "believe" in the post-Einsteinian "wave of space," "That the white bat universe flies," but also to "believe" that the double helix shape of DNA provides the "code" or model for physical anatomy and the shape and substance of intellect and emotion in man. Variations of the image of the "inky rider" permeate those poems in *Nearing the Millennium* that are philosophical. Throughout all three volumes, there are many references to twists and circles and curls and turns and bends and orbits.

Another ruling image that binds the trilogy together is that of earth as a globe externalized. The "big eyes" of mankind, once fixed on earth, can no longer look out on the universe with the impunity and smugness of existence at the center of the mystery. On the moonflights, man for the first time looked back on earth, and in the process, everywhere became the Center looking at the earth. That is the key theme in Skellings' "Moon Poems," which, incidentally, judging from their dates of composition, 1962–63, were ahead of Neil Armstrong's "giant step for mankind." But Skellings sees the beginnings of man's conquest of space as another way for the poet to balance the claims of the Two Cultures. Or, as the section called "Launch" of "Moon Flight" begins: "He will become excited. / Within certain limits." As a science-poet, Skellings will avoid the tonal extremes of the scientists blinded to the arts by their holy technology, and the poets who dabble with space travel with facile romanticism. Until there are balanced voices between the Two Cultures, Skellings sees that the moon landings and man's future exploration of space will result in a mood of deadened accomplishment, "He will pick up a pebble of the moon. / It will be like the end of any love, . . ." Or, as expressed in the concluding section of "Moon Flight" entitled "Terminal":

The thunder on the moon is silent.
It is no less there. Ask
Any of the moon's pedestrians.
He will smile the smile of

No one you know.

And then his lids will rise,
Like the doors on storm cellars,
And you will see emerge
The ancient look of the survivor,
Pupils wide with aftermath,
The mind's streets filled with leaves and litter,
Black homes,

And a snapped blue sparking.

An exploit that should have transformed man into an "emissary against dragons" has lapsed into immeasurable disenchantment.

Such a mood also pervades the "Last Man on the Moon" who lands on "one more foreign airport" and then succumbs to "The formula: mild disappointment over joy." And the probable cause of such ennui? "Having picked men / Of no imagination . . ." So begins "Moonflight II" with its indictment of the Space Agency and its ignorance of the techniques of the arts. Unless a dialogue begins between the Two Cultures, there will be no language to describe the greatest human adventure ever, of man trying to be more than a space animal at the mercy of quantum physics.

The discovery of such a language is the roots of Skellings' trilogy. What lights up *Nearing the Millennium* is the vision of an engineer. Skellings is ever fascinated with how things are put together and how they work. Such a vision also becomes the basis of the poet as architect. Some of Skelling's poems would make a mathematician envious. For example, the poem "He Says, She Says" consists of 3-line stanzas, each line having either 4 words or 4 syllables. Or, in the "Das Ich Erkenne," where 17 words are used twice as mirrors. Precision also shores up a long poem that deals with the collapse of civilization. The world of "The Hartford Circus Fire" is doomed because its foundation is one of extravagance. Like the poem's "rope walker," Skellings balances between the extremes of content and execution. Underlying the spectacle of a 3-ring circus fire is structure that is pure cool math. Of the 8 sections of "The Hartford Circus Fire," the exact middle sections (3, 4, 5 and 6) are in free verse, framed by 1 and 2 and 7 and 8 which are strict sonnets. But not all the trilogy is built on the sound and sense of science. Some poems are more freely conceived; some seem conciously to avoid weighty matters. Such poems as "Spider," "Jack Smith, Magician," "South Beach When," "Librarian" and "The Prom" are filled with wit for the sake of wit. These lighter poems are artfully placed among the more thematic ones, a device similar to "comic relief." But in the trilogy, the tonal alternation of light and serious is meant to provide the reader relief from sustained philosophizing about the workings of science. The voice of a science-poet must never lose itself in the didactic; if so, it would sound as absurd as those "Apes garrulous as / Hell, chatting with one / Another . . ." in the poem "Yerkish." Here the title refers to the computer language spoken by chimps at the Yerkes Primate Center in Georgia. Having fun with civilization also plays over "An Archeological Site in France," where Skellings suggests that the Cro-Magnons, who "chipped and carved from the blue-green ice" and made their caves into "pleasure domes," were richer artists than we.

But midway through "Yerkish," Skellings sounds his own tonal key: "Disorder / Makes humor, goes / The equation." Most of *Nearing the Millennium* thrives on images of the infinite disorder of the post-Einstein universe. All is flux, that echoes in many of Skellings' poems, as "On Instruments," with its "Flying universe of excited atoms / Spinning." Quantum physics has destroyed the concept of a world sitting "out there," and man's ultimate comforting vision, an objective reality outside himself, is gone. Einstein's God keeps playing with his dice, Einstein or no. Such metaphysical noise as infinite "disorder," so "goes / the Equation," must be countered with infinite "humor." When the persona laughs in *Nearing the Millennium,* he is laughing on the way to a metaphysical grave. Skellings' humor is one of desperation. Once a science-poet (or anyone) acknowledges that he is but a speck in a whirling universe, laughter is the best, perhaps only, mode of survival and the reader of such tonal poety is invited also to laugh along the way, so long as he doesn't mind the sound of a poet's dice.

But there is nothing aleatory about Skellings as the architect of his trilogy. Its content may be a one with universal flux, but its method is more akin to Newton than Einstein. Overall precision is the structural principle that spans and cements the three volumes. "Incantation," the first poem of the first volume, *Heart Attacks,* sets the pattern (to be duplicated in the third volume) of beginning the personal and romantic before enlarging the vision to include society and the whole of nature, until the ultimate attempt at sighting the self between the stars. But first the reader is introduced to the intimacies of a poet, reminiscing about his youth, with the romance of nature being epitomized by the image of a "ficus tree," an "Incantation" that ends with "Now all the dryads are dancing."

In a sense, Skellings is beginning his trilogy the way he ends it, by "Showing My Age." But this initial romance of "ficus" and "dryad" dissipates into a larger pattern of biological discovery. Therefore, *Heart Attacks* consists of poems of orientation. The emphasis throughout is on what it is like to be inside the "heart." Life, literally and figuratively, beats everywhere. Poems about animals abound. Nature is constantly in the forefront and biology remains the touchstone of experience. The "ruling image," as Alexander Pope of the Newtonian Age would have said, is the DNA. It is "The point of / Mystification" in "Crown." Just as Skellings or "Any demographer of cells and he will nod." Or, as "Hand Calculator" puts it: "You have to hand it to the chromo-/ Some," a "Living proof" that is more fully developed in the major poem, "The Double Helix," the "Spun thing / Center of all sun thing" sparked by the "inky rider." All this riding "On the ole D n A" is meant to orient the reader to a basic fact: that the DNA is the structural form that gives shape to everything the reader sees in an otherwise disorderly universe. From the "ficus tree" of "Incantation" to the "excited atoms" of "On Instruments" (a three-part final poem), *Heart Attacks* concludes with another D n A ride:

Spin out from the navel, spin
In from the stars, man is
Middling, the skin of the real.

and, meanwhile, none of the dryads have stopped "dancing."

Skellings' American trilogy concludes with the title poem of the third volume, "Showing My Age," which defines the limits of optimism and pessimism of a science-poet. But first, Skellings duplicates the architectural design of the first volume by beginning his third volume with a romantic splash of personal nostalgia, "Pruning Roots." But this poem is no mere imitation of the earlier "Incantation," because "Pruning Roots" bears the mark of the accumulative experience encountered in the middle volume, *Face Value*. In "Pruning Roots," the natural sciences have grown social along with the persona, who takes the reader on a Whitmanesque odyssey to discover the value of the person. People are now meeting other people all over America. The resultant poems are generally less philosophical. Orientation is now directed at, what the title indicates, taking things more at "face value." But Skellings is also an architect of titles that brim with irony. *Face Value* literally prepares the reader for a series of social portraits. But people are not things, and Skellings probes beneath "the skin of the real" to what is uniquely central to the individual. The "Librarian," the "Wallflower," the "Chaperone" and the many others are usually targets of satire, mostly bittersweet, never savage. The real "value" of the middle volume of the trilogy is how the satire never goes beyond the limits where a poet of science can no longer remain, essentially, human. This sets the mood and tone of "Pruning Roots." Unlike "Incantation," much on nature but void of any immediate human presence, the nostalgia of "Pruning Roots" is based on a personal encounter with the limits of family. Now the "ficus tree" is being felled before the human stage of the poem fill with a 77-year-old father and the "wife's whole family." Now toward the end, "Root sap cakes my sticky hands," the poet implies that his father must soon die and that he now finds it harder to leave his own roots. The social legacy of being on the American road in *Face Value* has now deepened and enriched the persona in *Showing My Age*. When Skellings re-establishes the architectural pattern of enlarging his vision from the personal to the public to the universal, he is now able to synthesize what he discovered about his and others' biological limits in *Heart Attacks* and sociological limits in *Face Value*. Thus, the title, *Showing My Age,* also works two ways. Skellings begins with his own inner weather and ends with the intellectual climate of our times.

His and our final coming of age consists of "21 Genes." These units of verse of the long "Showing My Age" are small congregations of verbal counterparts to those seed patterns that determine the direction of growth. Throughout these "genes," Skellings sets his verse on the forward edge of the latest speculations about the nature and evolution of intelligence. "'Man is bilaterally summetrical'." This belief in the ultimate consolidation of the respective functions of the split brain enables a science-poet like Skellings to discover his own mode of architecture. Throughout the "21 Genes" (and elsewhere in the trilogy) all references to twists and bends and turns and orbits and circles exemplify right hemisphere thinking in the brain, while verbal tricks and jumps in mood and tone exemplify left-handed activity. The esthetics of poetry have now entered the human brain. "The double helix of the hour's glass crosses / The infinity in a grain of sand." Skellings has begun this gene "17" with: "Mr. Moebius, my math is humming" because an assessment of the present and future growth of life must avoid the didactic. And so Skellings "hums" by adopting a jazzy style, "Bi *Helically* Symmetrical, Mama . . . Is what I say," figuratively, sounding left-handed about right-handed matters. The esthetics of the hemispheric brain results in rambling philosophical speculation conversational enough to bring the stars down to the street. But the esthetics based on the split brain also aim to start a dialogue between the two hemispheres, similar to the dialogue that will hopefully bring together the Two Cultures. This beginning of dialogue is the source of Skellings' optimism. The direction of human evolution (and human betterment) already seems to be "humming":

Right brain running the left side
Left brain crossing right
Oh corpus callosum
Meeting of minds

Those voices following Einstein may still set man as a speck in a universe of random curved light and flighty matter. The pessimistic side of Skellings agrees. But if that "Old splitbrain" ever "Come[s] to attention" within itself, then, amid all the excited plasma flying apart and running down to entropy, man will be the one speck running counter, up the evolutionary ladder like a Moebius strip, with one science-poet smiling along the way.

Ever since Keats lamented that "Newton destroyed the rainbow," American poets (and their British cousins) have decried the workings of science and technology. Such a belittling of the Other Culture seems all the more blatant as America, indeed, nears the millennium. During the latter half of the 20th Century, the ascension of America as the world's political power has coincided with an age epitomized by technology and its consequences. Yet the mainstream of American poetry continues to shun this vital sphere of our times. Instead, American poets seem content taking American experience at "face value." There has been a goodly amount of social criticism. But few of the ikons have fallen from the sky. Light remains straight and no dice rumble for them in the heavens. Space-ship earth, instead, turns into a family closet where many poets (following the lead of Robert Lowell) prefer to do their "life studies," munching on conversational tone and the most free verse, all about the "good old days." According to the tribe of Lowell, druids should "sing" in the family closet, not out where genes talk to the sun. With rare exceptions (such as the Archibald MacLeish poem on Einstein) current American poets have preferred the *status quo* between the Two Cultures, showing little or no awareness of the mysteries at the roots of physics, biology and other sciences. Thus far American poetry has, to echo the conclusion of Skellings' "Tectonic," "Ignore[d] news from the bone," and, in the process has not heard either the "news" of the corpus callosum at odds with an entropic universe, or the possibility of a resurrected rainbow.

—Reprinted from *The Massachusetts Review* 20, no. 1 (Spring 1979)

Acknowledgments

"At Sunland Training Center" appeared in *Miami Magazine*.
"The Double Helix" appeared in *The Florida Review*.
"The Hartford Circus Fire" first appeared in *The Massachusetts Review* and subsequently in *Fireland Arts Review* and the memorial issue of *The Hartford Courant*.
"Florida" was printed as a poster for *Geojourney* (Florida Department of Natural Resources).
"Heartwood" and "Friendly Game" first appeared in *Monument* (Arizona State University).
"Leavings" appeared in *Midwestern University Quarterly*.
"Welfare Shout" first appeared in *Florida Quarterly*.
"Artistic" and "Librarian" appeared in *Fireland Arts Review* (Bowling Green University).
"Melodramatics" appeared in *Bridge*.
"A Needle's Eye" first appeared in the anthology *West of Boston*.
"To a Beauty" appeared in *Metamorphosis*.
"Creative Writing Notebook" first appeared in the anthology *The Poet's Hand* (Maryland Library Association).
"For a Friend with Two Years to Live" appeared in *Gryphon*.
"The Tracks of Tyros" appeared in *Lillabulero*.
"Children's Verse" first appeared in *The Miami Herald*.
"How to Pick a Mistress, Or" and "Understanding is a Tone of Voice Blues" appeared in *The South Florida Review*.
"Sharpy" and "Owner" first appeared in *The Chinese Student Weekly* (Hong Kong).
"Projection" appeared in *The Iowa Defender*.

Heart Attacks
(1976)

Frost to Skellings,

Skellings to Frost, it's difficult
Across this dark. I remember, of all things,
Your tie, conservative, with a little pattern,
Tight about the neck of a boiled shirt
Sharp with starch. Everything matched.
And your thin white hair combed forward
In a residue of vanity. That night
You couldn't eat before the reading,
But got down some egg custard.
We had our picture taken. The bright
Flash burnt your old eyes and they watered.
Then you leant to my ear and whispered,
As if it were the inside of your soul,
"The bastards are killing me." Oh Robert,
I went on after you died, but never
Righted a wrong. It's been a long time
Since you took my arm and mumbled almost
Under your breath, "It's a big step."

Incantation

I keep coming to this chair
Today. Back and forth between
The ficus tree trailing aerial roots
Outside, and this chair.

Back and forth between
The tame wood and the free.

I am a hammock hung to the winds.
I am a sail today.
I strain as hard as I can and then
Go back to the measured tread again.

What can I start? My pencil breaks.
The ficus creaks with the breeze.
The chair creaks with my weight.

Axes, I threaten. I shall kindle
Some kind of blaze. You shall be
Food for fire if not thought.

The empty tree whispers of singing birds.
The emply chair is silent with its dead.

More, I shout, to the arching rafters.
The door shudders on its jambs.
The shelves under the books stiffen.
The table offers coffee.

Oh God, I hear the forests falling.
Timbers moan in the holds of the ships,
Spars sing in the wings of planes,
All the toboggans in the hills are rushing,
Skis are hissing,
The great woods of the world are howling.

The pines of the walls encircle me.
The polished years are shining like brown bones.

I sink into the chair.
The tree enters the house.

Now all the dryads are dancing.

At Sunland Training Center

After hearing a poem read slow
About snow
And holding the scraping
From a freezer
Melting through her hands
The mongoloid child says,

Snow is like wet pants.

We are aghast. Not only
Has this child thought, but
Made her own poem. Yes.
Snow is
Like wet pants, and we

Who have learned to walk, talk, not
Wet our under things

Wince at the arrogance
For it is not reserved to kings
The arrogance of our own
Power.

How fine and up right we are!
Only occasionally knocking
Things over, only once in a long
While tongue tripping.

Superb and splendid,
We chase the world well, only
Twice a month perhaps
Crying over spilt
Lives. Oh my, we never
Dreamed that we would finally
Know it all.

The child looks up again
And says so we will not forget,

Snow is like wet pants.

To His Machine

Are you still here,
Black thing of terrible teeth,
Humming and clacking?
Deep in, a developing growl.

Let me say
Your parentheses have ever
Been only part of the circle.

Some day all your asterisks will fall.
You'll end up in business
Or back to school.
Your numbers will be up.

Good riddance.
You have always been
Stingy with exclamation!

Dash it all, be kind.
And not too questioning.
Spell my name right and one night
I will free your carriage,
Release your margins.

I will buy you a red ribbon.

You can go and
Shift for yourself.

Crown

There is a spot
On the back of the head
That body and self spin round
And go down.

This is true. Ask
Any demographer of cells
And he will nod.

Some men go bald
There first, and some
Later, as emptiness
Creeps up from the eyes.

All of us know the spot
By feel, and I for one,
Confronted by questions
With no sides or bottom,
Reach up and rub.

It is some
Sort of answer. Rub.
Perhaps. Rub.
Maybe. Rub again.

At least we have found
The point of
Mystification. From there,
Who knows?

The Double Helix

I

When I am a ghost
Do not believe
In me

Believe
This blackness curiously lined on white

Interstices of thought and breath
Believe

Intervals in the struggle of the heart
Believe

This
Believe:

That a wild curve lit my mind
Was
Perhaps my mind

Retinal shadow of the surface of the world
Panned gold of the camera brain
Slits of the senses mere slits

Oh saddle shaped light
Oh inky rider

II

At tension
One thought in the chamber
He killed his dream

One simple idea he took
From no book
Put it to his head

Pulled its trigger

Fact
It spoke

And so he woke

III

We all rode many times
On the ole D n A

Up from the swamplands
Out of the sea

Ho ho honey
You rode with me

Now that you're here
All that behind

Down from the branches
To see what you find

Fear for your body
Hope for your mind

We all rode many times
On the ole D n A, et cetera

IV

Spun thing
Center of all sun thing
Wave of space

Galaxies like fish slosh
In you

That's a new twist
Said Mother Matter

E is M times me some way
Figured Light

Strain
Said Culture

No Yes
Said Brain

I am a sine
Origins pass by

That Time
Is running in

V

Woke to a code

IMPERATIVE CONTACT SELF
IMMEDIATELY FOR FURTHER
INTRUCTIONS STOP

Woke to a call:
It's me. You know. It's me.

Woke to this
Believe

That the white bat universe flies
And we ride its winging
In a wild curve in the cell
In a wild curve in the night

Know says the cell
What says the night

And the helix twists of infinity
And time is the turn of the twist
And the spine stems and the fingers leaf
And the eyes flower

Oh saddle shaped light
Oh inky rider

Fictions Personal

*"My right side is masculine.
My left side is feminine."*
—patient to R. D. Laing

You caught wise. Your truth sticks out
Like a sinister thumb.

What do you know of directions
In the twist of the genes,

The curvatures of the chromosome?
What do you know?

Insiders, those eastern meditators
On the Yin and the Yang,

Felt cross sections of all spines
Sunning their selves

Like cats arching. Or palms spinning
So slow only a seed could

Whisper wheres. Well, you caught me
Up. Strong as a Lear ramble.

Only thin covers separate our stories:
You next to me on the bending shelf.

Prices

Each year
The cost of paper
Grows more dear.

For you,
My Jewish printer says,
A deal.

He is full of inks
And watermarks.
His fat thumb riffles a ream.

This ought, he winks, to
Hold a poem.

How can I answer every
Poem is a raw
Deal,

Each word of the way
Illegible, unruled.

He cocks an ear to the press
And with the nail of an index finger
Tightens a screw one turn.

He cries to his devil,
Trim this even, then
Come back this evening at eleven.

All this while
The press is shouting,

Similar similar similar.

Up North

Here comes Summer with a bird in her throat
Sings some dumb poet from New England,
Who has waited the winter for a piece.

She *lives* in Florida, mate. You're only
Another fling. Who know her well tell
A whole other tale. Remember this, john,

She catches cold easy, begins about Miami,
One day a nip in the air notes a loss:
She'll take all her clothes and the hifi.

Get wise. She'll pop her dime down on
The ponies at Hialeah, lay herself
Hot on the beaches, follow the dogs.

I know you think you're a slicker,
Not a drop of naive left in the bottle,
But don't bug *me*. It was you got your hopes up.

Yerkish

It was all right with us
When they painted and people
Paid money to take home
Ape art. Money is
Partly funny any way.

Garish blotches with
Little control reminded
Us of our own art
Attempts. Disorder
Makes humor, goes
The equation. Who
Could ever get those
Long brushes to work
Right any way.

This, though, sets
The teeth on edge,
Apes garrulous as
Hell, chatting with one
Another, make the
Heart chill. God
Will most likely
Be brought up.

What then, any way?

He Says She Says

She says it is
A cinch. All you
Have to do is

Get on your toes
And turn. But when
I do I can

Feel muscle stretch.
He says one must
Limber one o-

Ver the other.
He says it is
A snap. I think

Near that word, too,
But do not speak
It in my head.

The book says don't
Struggle, but here
Even was a

Trouble. Who do
We do this for?
Do they think God

Is loose? Think His
Great joints will flex?
They say it's all

Matters of the
Posture. Let them
Go hang, thinking

Eli! Eli!
Surely something
Inside will give.

Oval

I am given a gift.
A butterfly and a flower.
A metaphor framed on a black oval.
How fitting.

I put it under the lamp's light,
Shining and artificial,
Trophy of some afternoon
Of love perhaps?
Or summer boredom.

For a moment I can feel the caterpillar
Aging and drying.
Colorful creature,
Have you had enough of dying?

I do not know, blue and brown,
What you are.

Let someone else call out your name.
Your name. Name.

And suddenly I am pressed, too,
At a thought of Yeats

Spreading magnificent wings.

Social Security

We argue, my father and I, about
Economics, though he calls it plain
Money. All are at the till,
He complains. "They"
Took everything good away.
Politician means on the take.
I, he says, worked every penny shiny.

Here, mother comes through
From the kitchen,
Her eyes raised significantly
To heaven.

Dad, I say, using the word
Fashionable when I grew up,
It isn't that way.
At seventy five you already
Have back more than you paid.

He says, I make them pay because
They made me pay. It's justice.

I say, the numbers of elderly
Have increased, thank
Modern medicine, and . . . But
I have brought up doctors,
A bloody mistake.

Those butchers, he shouts,
And my argument collapses
Like a vein.

Once long ago, before
Even any of my poems remember,
My father put his hand on my shoulder,
Which was going off to college.
He looked me in the blue eyes long
And said, Go learn more
Than your poor father.

I did, Dad. Does it do any good?

Conventions

Mr. Gravel uses Vitalis,
Or at least looks as though,
And he's a Senator, U.S.

I watch him on the tube,
Supporting native rights
And a supersonic airplane.

Remember, Mike, when I flew
Us around Alaska, the big
Rally in Nenana, that Eskimo

Covered with blue and orange
Buttons and drunk on your
Whiskey? When I asked him,

With a small grin on my face,
Who will *you* vote for?
He answered, Ralph Rivers.

I said, What the Hell
Are you doing with all
Those buttons for Gravel?

He said, They make good
Fishing lures under the ice,
And then he had the grin.

We've both flown a long
Way since then, Mike, but
Often my brow crinkles

Who attracted more fish
That season? Who tugged
Their hooks into nature tighter?

Crossing the Doral lobby
In Miami, you said, *You
Know, you're in show business,*

Too. I thought, then, of all
The speeches. And that orange
And blue lure, spinning coldly.

Treasures

Gramma came to the sunshine
State, brought by her daughters,
The blonde, the red, the black
Haired one. Away from the old
New England roots, now
Mouldering like forest mulch.

She sunned and hummed and then
Her mind began to slip.
One day they came upon her
Weeping for nothing. Why,
They fluttered, why?

My pretty box, she cried, with all
My treasures, gone for good.

But there was no box.
Later that night they learned
Her sister died away that afternoon,
The younger, the one she always
Took care for.

Not given to odd beliefs,
The daughters smiled.
An odd coincidence. Odd. Very
Odd, was the most wonder
They would own to, being modern.

Today that day came back
To her red haired daughter,
Now gone gray. And this gray
Head, my mother, tells
Me all of it. Tears, like little
Bifocals, help her read the past.

Long after she has left me
To myself, I keep my eyes tight
Till colors swarm. A pretty
Box appears. The lid is ajar.
There is nothing in the box.

Hemingway

Never quit
At a spot suitable,
He told us.

When he knew what
Would happen he
Put down his pen
And leaned back safe
With a head start
On tomorrow. Then

Was taken care of,
Characters
Frozen happening,
As if the film
Broke.

One early morning,
Sure what was next, he
Got up from his life.

The Leningrad Writers Conference 1942

for Yevgeny Yevtushenko

The starved had reached one thousand a day
With the temperature thirty below zero
And the writers had to burn their chairs
But they did meet and hold their conference

Zhenia, tonight I watched the old films
Of that Hero City holding out holding out
Holding out under months of shells falling
On homes with thick frost on the inner windows

And I thought of our first meeting in Alaska
With all the writers gathered at the college
And how we talked of poetry half the night
While outside the cold and the blackness waited

Zhenia, tonight I sit writing in Florida
Sipping from the simple white of cold milk
While the long breath of the air cooler
Settles over my shoulders like a shawl

And I hardly know what I am trying to say
Only that somehow the boiling heart
As well as the frozen bone must be held back
By poets who must ever keep their conference

Memory

Oh, these paper
Flowers are faded.
Though they did
Last a year
The sun got to them,

Man knows no dye
To fix forever.
Glass slowly goes.
And stain in woods.

Your words
Had sorts of colors
Once to make me
Wonder.

I'd hold them high
Long after they were
Over.

They have weathered so
I cannot tell if they were
Ever
Sweet or sour.

I rush to your photo.
Yes, the face too is turning
A little yellowed.

Now I am forced to flush
All old thoughts that were
Enameled.

And see whether.

Remembering Mailer

Provincetown:

After the afternoon sail
On the publisher's catamaran
We got ready for the
Big Party at Norman's

The sail was calm enough
The party loud enough
Drunk enough

And then they all went home
Telling stories

There was only one fight for
You to get into

One boy lay on the porch
And cried

We sat with the last
Half bottle of warm bourbon
To watch the dawn
Raise over Provincetown

Then everything was still

I praised Yeats and you said
I can rewrite anything
For the better

I opened the book
To one of many
Turned down corners

You said flat
I'll be damned if I don't

Well,
Damned if you didn't

Then we were silent, too,
Over what had just happened

And a huge fireball
Rose from the water

Another Oval

Hair soft about her oval face,
She says, You don't talk
Right in a poem,
I mean, a poem goes
Different.

I answer, Tell me
More.

She says, hair tossing
Soft about her oval face
It just, well, like, it
Sort of dances.

I answer, Let's dance
Then.

She says, Oh you.

An Archeological Site in France

This find this dig will last them years
Hard by a cliff where once a river ran
Melt from the foot of a glacier now
Perched on the top of the spinning globe

Thirty students of assorted sex
Living together for two summer months
Under the direction of careful professors
Casually dine beneath their canvas tents

Each day unearths more evidence of men
Much like ourselves in stature and in aim
Though in a colder climate under a harder sun
But now the students wash and clean their teeth

During daylight the sable brushes work
At bone and flint uncovering bit by bit
Layer under layer under layer of those lives
Revealing masterpieces of conjecture

Even the cigarettes of those who smoke
Are delicately stubbed and pocketed
As well as paper wrapper from chewing gums
Or tissues from hapless students who caught cold

They eradicate each hint about themselves
At the end of a day labor before
Precise cameras wheel in and align
To document the tight terrain they work with

And slowly the remarkable portrait grows
Of how the culture called Cro-Magnon man
Mated and hunted and played and died
And because it shows his soul made art

Some mornings miraculous discoveries
Hard and clinging clay is scalpeled off
And as old as Genesis sculptured in bone
A white ten thousand year old mouthless face

Two necklaces have so far been disclosed
Whose rawhide thongs have long since disappeared
Each shell and tooth together in location
That makes mere chance position beyond chance

That same day found ornate abstract engravings
Whose meanings are entirely unknown
Although analysis by a specially set computer
Implies the nicks make calendars of the moon

One professor having turned the finds for decades
Offers these non-industrial people might have
Painted and carved and inscribed pictures
Purely for entertainment in the winter

Two giant elk of course by now extinct
Are represented in one totally fine example
Which uses the cave rock face itself
To emphasize the muscles of the elk and ibis

And one wall painting rests at the far end
Of a cave within a cave where the painter
Must have lain with his right arm extended
As far as he could reach with a long brush

It is completely in the utter darkness
And the man or woman must have brought a fire
Or else have traced the animal outlines
Without ever seeing the finished features

Which shows how intimately the artist
Knew the anatomy of the animal or else
There may be some perfected explanation
That lies beyond our knowledge at the moment

Hair seems to have been quite important
And braids of every sort adorning statuettes
Are rendered in exaggerated detail
As well as the usual giant phallic features

The flint tools that were used for carving
Can even today be made by patient hands
And an old professor with time to kill
Has imitated the production of an axe

We might even postulate a shrine
In an area far back in a particular cave
Creatures half-man half-beast exist
Proving they had a certain imagination

Red ocher with which they brightened statues
On ritual day may still be found in crevices
And curlicues upon the little figures
Although the form of the rites is not yet clear

Some shapes are very obviously totemic
Meant to gather power for the hunter
In order that he be more than a match
For any angered beast he might encounter

One enterprising painter used a natural hole
Already present in the rocky wall
As the eye of a bison in full run
And the eye even now seems quite alert

New questions promise clearer answers
And we can only wonder what they may
Have chipped and carved from the blue-geeen ice
And set up in these caves to worship

Animals life size and larger
And also beasts we have no record of
That peopled their primitive lives and thoughts
Smoothed into miracles by their own warm hands

The students often let their minds so roam
About the valley after the evening meal
While the professors read and happily argue
And the same style continues at Lasceaux

Extrapolation

Most of us is math, which comes as no
Surprise: The limbs of trees circle
The trunk, leaves the branch, all
Spin slowly the great tap root. This
Can be seen from palm frond about
The nut, arms and legs popping from
The spine, twinned brains blooming.

Go down deep and you hit math. Every
Time. Darwin shaped it up by
Statistics. A natural arithmetic.
He stopped there, but because each
Poem should have one great idea,
Here: Extrapolation is genetic.
That should account for you, big eyes.

Naturalist

This peaceful lake
Of Central America harbors
Such odd creatures

As the Yellow Spinesnake
And you see him now
Upright on lilypads
His yellow hood spread
Like a bright umbrella

He feasts on the pad frogs
Catching them midair
At the exact top of their leap
But now you see him
In the strange erect
Twining of mating

For all the world
Like a medical wand
And there hops

Andrew's Lacewing
A very intelligent bird
Who can swim with his wings
And leaps
Out of the water for

Now in slow motion

The giant dragonfly

And remarkable for a bird
Builds his nest half under water
With rushes and watery weeds
Giving birth to its young live

And here you see the Brown Rockfish
Who backs into caves and crannies
Expanding himself till his mouth
Seals open the opening
And then he waits for
Minnows

Each of these remarkable species
Eats its own young
Which is common
Only at this lake

Perhaps only in our time

History
May look at us from these
Camera angles

Too and find
Our camouflage wanting
Under its infra
Red

Science Fiction

Take an animal almost extinct,
A huge hairy beast that, threatened,
Gathers his young in a circle,
Facing outward, for all the world
Like a herd of soldiers surrounded.

Suppose this animal intelligent enough
To dig through deep snow for grasses,
Bright enough to slide open doors,
Lift latches to escape from enclosure,
Loyal to companions of other species.

Imagine a man. Taught to love money
And automobiles and girls and all
Else Americans hold dear. Imagine him
Of good stock with a fine inheritance,
Married to a woman of impeccable looks.

Imagine him educated in finance,
Economics, the history of cultures.
Imagine him suddenly choosing the Greeks
Over the Romans, suddenly spending
His entire fortune to capture the animals.

Suppose he suddenly sees,
With his mind's eye, Man as another animal.
Suppose he barely glimpses, at first,
As heat waves trouble the vision
Of a field of grasses, that all

Animals are equal. And, for a moment,
The man sees with the eyes of the sun.
Suddenly all is simple, his life clear:
He will domesticate this beast,
The first for a thousand years.

Yes, that would be a story,
If we had a man like that, a hero
Of only his own battle. Picture him
Large, with massive features, picture him
An American with a mind of his own.

Simplify the scene. See him and the herd
Facing each other on an infinite plain.
Hear him talk low to the animals,
Then soft to himself, "I will find
The right men to take care of you,

"Men almost as extinct as you,
Who will care for you as they
Care for themselves. Who will never
Touch your meat. Who will pull fleece
For weaving the lightest down clothing."

Picture that and you have my story.
Imagine him finding those natives
And taming those beasts, and see,
At the last, the bond between man
And animal so tightly knit

That the animals protect around him
As they do their very own.
Ask yourself if you are not moved
By this portrait, somewhere beneath
Your heart, behind your postures,

Behind your lies to yourself that
There are no men like this, that
The story is impossible, that
No one would write a tale like this
With his whole life. I will not argue.

I will go aside and read from a book.
And if you do not believe in books,
I will bring you North, to the edge of land,
And show you the great dark animals grazing
And the natives carding their wool.

Epilog

for my friend John Teal

Blunt, bluff handed, he
Can be accused of
Having befriended animals,
A silly vice in such an age.

Add to that.
Unpardonable sinner, he
Has also befriended Man,
A foolish flaw in any age.

But he goes on and odd,
And it is no surprise
That in that way
He has befriended God.

From the Striped Chair

It has arrived again,
Caterpillar season, only
This year I do not get the
Broom, sweep cocoons
From the screen, tidy
It all. Instead,

I swig at the half
Bottle of vodka left,
Let the world spin.

This yellow one, I
Spy on him from my side
Of the plastic veil.
All is insect green
And perfect, he
Thinks. Mouth
And mouth, something
Tells him, and it
Will blossom right.

I know that call, heard
It young. At least
By the age of
Reason. It did, then.

But I tell you, bundler
From the sun, truster
In future beaty, that
Won't do now.

Sequel

One day past my warning,
Friend, and in an orange
Flash, you are plucked
By an oriole.

Too soon flying,
Food for chicks,
How is that deep slumber
Now?

If it comes, let it be
In our sleeps,
Dreaming of a tomorrow
Lovely in color,

All sex and wings.

Amulet

Wary to keep
Front hooves from the mud
The young buck at the waterhole
Has already been singled
By the yellow grasses.

The grasses watch him drink,
A nerve in his neck flicking.
Quick, the antelope jump
Running and gone.

The lion leaves the carcass
To lap some water. Then she drags
A path in the grasses.

I watch from a spot
Even more secret. I will scratch
On a small stone a hoof
Under a tooth
And over both

Power bites fear.

Surface Tensions

The blades of the wooden oars leave
Circles in circles,
The water parts at the prow,

These are strange waters.

What prowls, terrible and terrific,
Brooding?

The light line I cast in the night
Tremors, tugs,
Goes bottom in a whine, the twine

Smokes, the boat
Dips,

And line boat and man go under.

Who wins in this fishing?
We struggle in the dark,
Lung and gill gasp,

Element against element.

I nail a huge trophy on the wall,
Wet and dripping.

Look how his jaw mouths teeth work
Slimy inaudible words.

Listen to how old his sigh.

His drowning is my poem.

Grizzly

The Toklat grizzly
Is so smart
You end up being hunted.

So much for smart.

Boulders, thick brush,
Anything to conceal
Our motives.

Guess again.
There are some things
That stalk our world
That will not be put off.

They have the scent.
Step lively.

Tout

Here
Give me a leg up

Thanks
Now in the fifth
This is a good filly

And in the eighth
Top Spot is your best bet

You know
Gave my last wife
The same tip yesterday
She won't go for it though

After a while you can tell
The people who chance it
And those who pick

The favorite to show

The Elbow Room

A riotous old fellow
Came into the bar today

He said chief the job
Is getting *to* me

I need to use the pay phone
Call up a girl I know
Or something

At forty three
You never know whether
The old engine
Will kick over
Cold mornings

Got to stay in touch

And these hours
Are doing me in
All day hanging walls

Why in hell this sudden
Privacy? If I had my way

There'd be no more
Partitions give us

A beer your honor
Give all of us
A beer these wages

Make a man think

Home Made Candy

Pride first I suppose
Or perhaps
Names are a sort of spell
Put on a product

Aunt Jemima's
Duncan Hines'
Howard Johnson's

Then as the business grows
The name dwarfs the man

Imagine having a cake
Named after you
Or ice cream melting

Not at all like an automobile
Though that's getting closer

And no nickname will ever stick
Dunc Hines or Howie J. won't do

Nor does Mr. seem appropriate

This naming and claiming
Must go on I guess

We all want to get up in the world

So I have recently decided
To place on the roof of my house
In at least neon

Skellings' Red Hot Poems

[The red hot will flash on and off]

Shooting Match

Suppose one day you find yourself
Against the wall or a post
Hands tied behind and blindfolded.

Just suppose. And say
The resplendent officer offers you
A puff on a cigarette and you don't
Even smoke.

Or say he gives you a last few words
Which is extremely unlikely
But you have nothing in mind
Except nothing.

This is of course only supposition
For really they put a black bag
Over your head.

Up till then they tell me the condemned
Can't take their eyes off the pistol
To a man.

So you never truly get any last words
Unless you lie in bed and even then
Most times nobody listens.

For actually dying is a living hell only
For very literary persons who like
A neo-classical neatness.

Who prefer their symphonies finished.
Life tidy. No poem ending in
And . . .

The Hartford Circus Fire

A poem recalling the great fire
of Ringling Brothers Circus in
which hundreds of children were
burned to death. This ended the
outdoor tent circus in America.

toward the construction of mystery:

Al, the Phoenix, who each matinee
Lunched on coal and kerosene would say
This should have been his tale to tell. He'd bitch
If he grew hoarse and someone did his pitch.
Al never tumbled to the gift he lacked
And tried to tell the truth about his act,
As if the real were wonderful. The fact
Got him a small house. Then, burnt, he burned.
Confusion was a truth he never learned.
The last time that I looked, for once, his eyes
Were bigger than his stomach. Al went wise.

If you'd be barker for yourself, begin
Most carefully at pitching your "come in!"
For some will call all circuses a sin.

toward the construction of entertainment:

Small seats. Oh how we packed them in.
Not since Obadiah and Old Bet
Have towners crowded to the till to get
Their folded spieled away. Hearts lost within,
All else was given freely, for the lights
That glittered in their minds from sequined tights
Spun sweets on which imagination fed.
The eye was almost pipered from the head.

Small seats. While each one counted elephants,
We counted cash, and sunned our skins with dreams;
In floral winter quarters, warmer schemes
To round out a rich season with the tents.
We had a fine blue sky that no cloud crossed.
We glowed in our desires. We were all lost.

clown white:

The tumblers had gone off, when smoke
Rose, and a cloud
Of laughter
Rose immediately after.
An old joke touching a young crowd:
A flimsy house, a loud alarm, a shriek.
None of the clumsy volunteers could speak.
Hysterically falsetto, one throat screamed
Oh save my child!
The red truck rang its bell and then went wild.
On rubber feet, with giant toes,
And gripping tightly his prop hose
Stood spotlighted and fixed a man
Who was a clown, whose features ran.

cage:

Behind the booted man who claimed
There was no beast he hadn't tamed
A yellow mane of fire roared.
He spun, thrust to those jaws the scored
Rungs of a painted stool
That kept a hundred cats in school
Then like a fool
Forgot his rule
And ran, but Oh the sawdust floor was slick
And Oh that licking cat was quick.
He fell. And the stiff whip
Went limp and melted in his grip.
Down fell the planks. The flames flew up.
All at once his blanks blew up.

rope walker:

Above the crowd,
As usual, proud,
Alone, aloof ,
He'd brought his courage to the roof.

But now upon the wire and bar
An animal in fear he stood,
Devouring fire in his wood
And at his feet a pit of tar.

His act? To somersault through air
Once twice thrice and burst
Through a red paper square.
Oh Jack be nimble, Jack be quick,
Your thin air grows dark and thick.
He took one last impure breath,
Balancing how a flier dies.
Then he left the bar, and then
Once
        twice
                thrice.

side show:

Anger, the old tattoo,
Flooded his heart,
Rivered his veins,
And rivaled all the blue man's art,

Courage, the old measure,
Knew its pleasure,
Dwarfed the tall man, tripped him up.

Fear, the black barbell,
Fell. In that thunder
The strong man weakened and went under.

Then Fate, the lucky hick,
Swept the arcade:
Knocked down bottles, rang the bell,
Guessed each man's weight, and the right shell,
Saw through the skin show, did so well
He won all prizes. Quick,
He took his pick.

toward the destruction of elegy:

Small stones. As if the measurement of death
Consisted of some marble magnitude.
But better this for monument than crude
Trapping on a page with a black breath.
That could turn the sourest tongue more sour.
To see thought stiffen and contort can be
Too excellent a reminder of an hour
Already rendered much too readily.

Small stones. This deep remove
No man can quarry and no word can prove.
If all the answers tendered and applied
Curved firm containers for the tears we've cried . . .
But no schemes from philosophies apply.
A child has fashioned no pat way to die.

toward the destruction of luxury:

To lose what we had learned from what we saw
We sift through rubble for an unburnt straw,
But there are none. No, we had never guessed
Our civilization weak as all the rest;
We had built on sand on purpose, we
Used insubstantial fabric to keep free,
To stay precarious. That was the key,
We thought. Spend life within our lavish tents
And raise illusion through extravagance.

But ropewalkers had flipping hearts. Too bad.
Our clowns were wept and giggled out. Too bad.
The trainers had not tamed themselves. Too bad.
We should have known it of a canvas town.
It is a short time till the show's torn down.

Warning

April May June doesn't matter
Here much. The sameness
Outside, the similar months,
Slowly outwit Darwin and shape
The innards. The night sky fills
With words. It seems everyone is
Advertising.

The tourists make little
Of it. They expect strangeness
From any foreign city and are used
To adjusting.

At five, after the beach, the white
Clouds darken and there is rain.
Over our liquor we watch it
Fall. Almost time to shower again
And dress for dinner.

Far out above the sea a yellow
Bolt jags to the water. It
Is so far away not even it
Startles. Don't stay too long.

We say you get sand in your shoes.

Even America

Rust is at
My car

Mist from the sea
Certainly

The welcome light
At the front
Out

The bulb probably

Now the typewriter growls
In its bearings

I understand even America
Suspects its innards

So travel ends
So close neighbors
Stay away

I have had enough friends
And other foreign places

If new flames arise
Alive from the old fire

We'll keep dry
And lucky

We got it all in

On the Patio

An ant riot
At the coffeecup

A whole rimful of runners

It has got so one
Ought not put anything down

In fact they act as if
This the last taste of sweet

In their world

Enough to panic over

An ant economist might add two
And two together and figure

Another run on supply

See his society behave
Like no tomorrow

Were there a way
I would offer God knows
Tomorrow will see Him here

As usual
Leaning back thoughtful

For He remembers even
Yesterday

The Tanks of Amherst

The twin Cadillac engines roared
To my foot, while above
The turret whined electric,
Pointing the cannon over the pond.

Two girls ran to us from Memorial Hall,
Carrying sandwiches. We yawned
A hatch and they clambered in.

A joyride.

Up highway one sixteen toward Mount
Sugarloaf we clattered, then
Off the paved road up the hill
Under the apple trees, the
Experimental trees with grafted
Fruits from hybrid blossoms.

We chose the Delicious.

It was between wars. We shut
Down the engines and sunned
In the weak Spring shine,
Reserve officers training.

Later we rolled the great green
Thing next to the main road
To track the cannon on passing cars,
Fun to watch the fearful civilian
Faces under our power. With clear
Periscope, we looked far

Into the distance.

Today, another war has ended.
The night news shows rows of tanks
Hard beside foreign highways,
Empty hulls, cannon askew.

At home, relaxed, once again
The nation rests between actions.
The trees that bred true, bud.
Summer is about to bloom.

Peace will cover the apples.

The Collected Me

The *Miami Herald* has arrived
Too late to do any good.
From here disaster is trivial
And too far away, opinion
Already becoming brittle.
I am not ready for today,

Neither. Back in the studio,
I gather my old poems about me.
I could make a suit of them
And do a wild little dance,
But somehow I am not ready for
Collection and publication,

Neither. What is this
Being trapped in the morning?
After toast, before coffee.
Even the weather in the west
Seems only impending. No,
There is no sense in the moment,

Neither. The newsboys are now
Way up the street with their
Burdens. The mailmen have yet
To order their day together.
Between is the word for it.
A blank flyleaf between covers.

Tomorrow, I promise, I will
Gather my wits and sort out
The rubbish, staple the good
Times, discard the trash.
I may even search out the
Meaning of history. Tomorrow.

A Bare Walk

She goes

To the garden every day
Though no roses bloom
At this shade of year

Though these seasons
The world is brown leaf
And black thorn she goes

The world will turn
And longstem tea and climber
Rose will turn

To color of old flame
And fire with scents of old
And green wood smoking

For the rose has learned
To last through its own burning
Of slow summer and flash
Blazes so

Since she has learned
A sister glow
And burn she goes
To the garden

If all past autumns teach
The leaf were learned
At root and taught to turn
Of petal she would go

And winter

Movements

for Jules Pagano

On the ride to the airport
All the young men were silent
Fidgeting thick buckles
Fingering straps
Some mumbled prayers
Doing a clumsy penance perhaps

Inside the aircraft more silence
Deeper and more still
As if a storm gathered
Under the engines thunder

A moment in the doorway to
Emptiness a pause
Then the long float
Of timelessness

In the truck back
Everyone talked a mile a minute
All telling about the personal
Hands waving like little flags
Private fourths of July
Suddenly public and splendid

Later on in my life I raced
Automobiles around corners
As fast as I could and faster
Till one spun and the tires screamed
I would never catch up

And later I dared myself to solo
My own plane in the Arctic
Black mountains moving by in the night
With the soft glow of instruments
Feeling for signal direction

It is something about finding yourself
Alone on the rushing background
It is something about losing yourself
In your own wide pondering
And even now and here on this travel
Casting for orientation or fix of some
Incredible angle or curve or even
hint of location

As I cascade down the language
Hunting the one spot solo only
Where the hunting rests and the hunter
Meets himself smiling and easy

Cavendish

Others saw water: lakes of blue and the blue
Green ocean charging in foam on the sand.
Water, they knew, was most of a man, but
Then Cavendish found Hydro-gen, making
From fire, water. Water became clear.

Pools under trees, fresh wells, most
All creation sang anew. Cavendish withdrew,
A shy man, fearful of womanly currents.

Shy to the point of dying. From his bed
He ordered the watchers away, choosing
His own company at the last. The
Better to reflect? Afraid of his sighs?

He should give all of us pause, this
Divider of seas greater than the dreams
Of Moses, testing, who knows, even Death.

Monday at the Airport

About to fly I pass some airport time
Digesting the science of the month
Where one practitioner discloses
The universe is mainly a charged gas
And tells me with I sense a grin
Things are hardly solid
Compared with the hearts of stars

I must confess I never knew
They had a heart oh let alone
The sweet green earth might not
Support our every step

That one fine day the smiling adventurer
Might stride out his front door
And quite within the realm
Of possibility sink
Up to his knees in molecules
Stuck home forever

    Or worse
Two lovers just about to kiss
Would find they'd fallen through
Each other and what they posited
As terminal and stiff
Was insubstantial evanescence
Love a dream less real
Than life under anesthesia
And all their lies about how soft
The other quite come true

Oh my my flight's about to leave
Though now these second thoughts
Gather like nimbus clouds
What if the air won't actually
Hold a poet up for long?

When I look inside there is no
Heart of a star and it has
Been proven time and again
Thinner stuff prevails

Well what if it won't?
My trusting nature will
Take a deep breath of a charged gas
And charge: let's make believe
For one more day and let's pretend
For one more trip we

Can pursue the usual as usual
Can navigate the normal normally
And I for one must once again confess
Putting my travel folders down
I never really considered the far stars
I never truly flew beyond the moon

Series

When Francois Vieta invented the unknown,
Saying for the first time, Let X
Equal it, oh, the mathematicians
Scurried smiling. Here was a tool.

And after Leibniz got busy with his binary,
Our machines gabbled, Oh one,
What do you know?

Now we confront irrational numbers.
The counters ask, How intense
Is this or that idea of infinity?

Somehow we seem no closer, if in fact
We are now almost to the last decimal.
History awaits a final name. Who's Who
Will have nothing left to carry over?

Hand Calculator

Two, four, sixteen, two fifty six,
Six five five three six, and off
Scale, says my electronic mathbox.
I can't get that high by myself.
Things never have squared easy.

Five, says the right hand. Same
Here, says the left. Evidently
Hands knew number before the brain
Noticed. Like my calculator, it
Was built in. Living proof.

You have to hand it to the chromo-
Some. Not only has it hit
The right answer, but it shows
Its work. Look around at the
Classroom, by God, all earth and air.

On Instruments

by dial

The world on his windows changing,
The aviator corrects his blindness
With ever closer approximations
On space so perfect only radios
Define the course and curves
And even these bend imperfect.

No pilot holds his truth true
For more than divisions of instant
Where time itself is suspect,
Inconstants on a background
Inconceivable even to a heart
Keeping its own approximations.

He comes to love it. He can feel
Invisible wings holding. It
Registers fulfilment never
Absolute or ever completely
Rewarded or finished in anything
More than a nearness to plan.
Then, finally, the land.

He sips caffeine, shutting
His speeds down, relaxing as
Gauges leave his retinas,
After images subsiding, and
The quick math fades, too, as
Constants suitable only for this
Part of the whole route fade. The real

Turns real. A waitress smiles.
He finishes to leave again.

by bell

The meditator starts his journey
With a delicate thought touching
The bud of the navel, and knows
How the nut commands its leaves
To bush, how the circling flower
Explodes to small then larger fruit
Which fall to independence.

His travel begins in a double
Center revolving itself
And then the double doubles
Curves like planets take and suns
Swing out and away to courses
Forming arms of galaxies and
Clusters of fingers, orbits of eyes.

He comes to love it. He can feel
The mind turn softly about itself,
Tasting organ, blood, and gland.
The very brain doubles its halves.
Hands clap a together metaphor.
The toes tap iambic pleasures.

All without moving. Only attention
Bells, enclosing interiors,
Wheeling away from the center navel,
Each cell touched on the path,
Each vision visited, each
Tangent turned to expansion.

The man is spun, he knows. The world
Insides itself. He stays.

by shell

The double helix springs outward
And inward. Galaxies of cell
And sun unwind their helices.
And what towards? Both cell and sun
Are shell. The path is clear. Grow.

The traveler is water. It could
Be plasma, a cloud of molecules,
Flying universe of excited atoms
Spinning. Then man is hydrogen.

Spin out from the navel, spin
In from the stars, man is
Middling, the skin of the real.

Face Value

(1977)

Opening Shock

One is never prepared for it:
Although you clench the whole body
And even count the seconds off,
Whacko! Who would think silken cloth
Could stop you in midair so hard, so
Sudden is the word, like bone
Popping. And it can take the heels
From the boots, watch from the wrist,
Zippo through the pocket bottom.
But we never cursed the old T-Seven.
Laughter as it let us down from heaven.

It's natural as being born, our sergeant
Wise cracked, checking the umbilicals.
See, I remember each and every detail.
NO STEP, stenciled the wing in warning.

God. Was the sky *blue* that morning.

Dass Ich Erkenne

Yes, it's your old Whether
Man again, Ed Skellings
Here. Only poet writes
With both hands, folks,
Only poet with no poem about
Mirrors. But

Rectification is at *hand,*
Chillun, is at
Hand. Now

Consider your average electron
Trapped by powerful magnets
And levitated, yes,
I said *levitated*
In an energy well. Well,

Nick that little charged
Particle with a microwave,
Nick one direction, nick
The other, measure gently
La difference, and voila

One has this measurement.
And if, which is where the
Whether comes in,
I say and if
One uses the positron
For a quick comparison,

Well! We all will see
If matter and antimatter
Are exact mirror images
Exactly. And if not

Oh oh. If explodes,

Whether evaporates,
Metaphor won't and
Bye bye Aristotle.

Tectonic

Damned town is mined,
They mutter in Cumberland.
Most all Maryland balances
On worms of tunnels.

Come long hot summers,
Fairbanks will sink
Through the permafrost,
Spits the sourdough.

And at Miami, adds a cane,
The sea seeps salt
As we suck up fresh. Tap
Tap. Shaky Frisco!

We grow disturbed
For a moment, sit
And muse a minute.
But then we settle,

Forget what volcanos
Murmur, mumble, bubble
Over hell ever under.
Pave away, bulldozer,

Path to a further city:
We'll get the wig rewoven,
Not hear the heart's trouble,
Ignore news from the bone.

Extra Extra

I just found out Richard Nixon
Made TV commercials selling himself
Paid for by Abplanalp's money
Which Abplanalp made from royalties
On his patented aerosol valve
Which is obsolete because of the ozone.

On top of that this late president
Appeared on millions of TV screens
Once again selling himself but now
To the whole world as he stepped
Up on the Great China Wall.

And at that identical moment
Another large cash contributor
Named Howard Hughes was hiding
In a penthouse suite in Nicaragua
While Nixon was carried live
By the Hughes TV network.

And now I suppose you are angry
With me because this poem doesn't
Rhyme or have a moral.

Bicentennial History Lesson

Adolph was dissatisfied. He ordered
The priceless Gobelin tapestries
Torn down. In the last bunker
All walls would be raw concrete.
Waving his Walther, he directed
The removal of the final vestige
Of ostentation. Eva came then,
And the two of them settled in.

When Churchill slipped away
From the meeting on a whim
To visit Berlin (waiting for Joe
Stalin's slow train to cross Poland)
Winston stopped at the top step,
Then descended almost one flight,
Then slowly came back up out
From the bunker. His aides
Found three iron crosses,
Took two broken pieces of marble
Tabletop, and one torn paper
Scrap of the wall map of the world.

Even Harry Truman couldn't
Resist, and he slipped away,
Too, and his Chrysler convertible
Crossed and re-crossed the path
Of Churchill's Rolls-Royce
As they took the same expensive
Tour. His aides pocketed two
Iron crosses and three marble
Chunks big as a fist to use,
Back home, as paper weights.
That day, back home, in New
Mexico, a bomb had gone largely off.

That day, on the other
Side of the round world,
The Emperor sat imperially alone,

Defying generations of custom,
Awaiting the Prince to whom
He would order surrender.

Now you know what I know.
Some of us are less, some more
Than two hundred years old.

1976 Florida Almanac

With fourteen deepwater ports
Florida is unequaled in facilities
For water transportation, says
The almanac, as if everyone didn't know.

One does find out things, though,
About the number of
Surgical-Medical Misadventures:
Seventy-three. And that two died
Of high and low air pressure,
Probably one each. Did you know
The California Poppy blooms
March to June, is hardy,
Re-seeds and volunteers readily?

Four hundred eighty-eight persons
Dropped dead in unspecified falls
From unspecified heights, pushed
By no one specified. Think of that.

The Tangelo is a hybrid, naturally,
And its orange-tangerine
Only really good for out-of-hand eating.

Florida has all the necessary
Ingredients for cement, imagine.
And all United States production
Of staurolite is confined here.
No diamonds we know of. Large
Quantities of gold off shore.
Forged in pieces of eight.

No American Indians were
Expelled from school in any county
During the whole of Nineteen Seventy-Three.
How exemplary.

Murder statistics are in the back.
For obvious reasons. Everyone
Has something to hide, but
Twenty-three under the age of five?

And increasing? Your average felon was
Twenty-four, Baptist, came
From a broken home, was
Occupationally unskilled, had
No priors, got four years.

The University of Florida plays There
Home Home There Home There There.
The University of Miami simply plays.

And if everything runs true in '76
The hounds will run at Flagler,
The horses at Gulfstream Park.
Six hundred and fourteen people will drown.
Fifty-seven inches of rain will
Fall in Dade County.

Raccoon, beaver, bobcat, Key Largo
Wood rats, and all reptiles
Other than alligator will go
Once again, unprotected.

The state will go Democratic.
The beaches will continue to erode.

Alaska

I suppose it was the picture of Frenchie,
Toothless grin, leaning on the big radial
Engine of the Cessna with the broken prop,
Broken ski, shack in the background,
Rusted oil drums scattered everywhere,
I suppose it was the picture of Frenchie.

But I have tossed aside the book on politics
And I am flying once more in the Bush
Past that huge white rock of the sky
That the Eskimo call The Great One,
And I skid down again at Talkeetna
To drink hot coffee in the one cafe.

I suppose it was the picture of Frenchie,
Long lost by the time I found him,
A photo in a flight shed in Nenana,
That moved into my mind while reading
Out of doors in the perfumes of Florida.
I suppose it was the picture of Frenchie.

On the Death of Your Father
for Glenn Goerke

Birth and death share the same
Smell, Glenn, you said,
Looking for some
Simile, some
Comparison, some
Way of making the thing clear.

My friend. There is no
Way. Nothing will ever be
The same. Death
Is definition.

Adams, Jefferson, those great
Fathers died on this day.
Who can think on them? Personal
Grief flares like a rocket. We feel
The house divided.

We say, thank heaven he
Suffers no longer. Finally
We sigh, it is over.

We know a lie, having lied
Before. This is a lie.
We taste even a good lie
On our lips. Truth is

He should have gone on forever,
And we should go on forever,
Let all else lapse.

Outside, a nation's fireworks
Explode, proclaiming
Celebrations of our liberty.

You and I know we live in chains
Of flesh. Liberty is for a time
And in a place. Birth and death
Have no smell. They are words
For the living.

History clamors for another man,
Hungering, unsatisfied,
Another man, another man.

Let fools try to console you.
They have always known
What is essential and necessary.

But listen to my poem whisper,

Our bones make the past real.

Male Lead

for Burt Reynolds

They make you who you never thought you'd be.
And then they fall in love with it.

No telling who you might have really been.
Or still might be.

You work becoming someone else
With the care and delicacy of a spy.
Learning your lines, you mutter
To whatever self you are today,
Let me see now. Where was I?

You play a king.
And each night are dethroned.

Each night, like a real cop,
Turn in your badge.

Tomorrow all the action scenes:
The fight, the roof, the long chase
Down the clanging fire escape.

Much later some director
Will edit your imitation life together.

You watch a hand performing autographs.
Which role is signing this year?

You are your own talk show host
And deadpan to the mirror,
Be Yourself!

Alone, no one is Hero. No one The Lover.

The world still snarls in its toughest way,
Get this straight.

And always the hidden writer sighing,

Say after me. Say after me.

Radio John

for John Eastman and WIOD Miami

Your voice is dark as the night
We listen in.

One o'clock is always hungry
For company. And for many
And for more each year
That black phone is the only wire
To anyone.

Ring me, ring me, ring me,
Goes the bell. John,
You're always there.

We'll talk of love long distance
And at night time rates.

We'll tell the time of our lives
And how we almost drowned in it.

We'll chat of hate, we'll
Listen in on others
Who give themselves away.

We'll say (but softly to ourselves)
That guy makes sense.
That lady is a nut.
That poor man needs a friend so bad
He makes me *mad*.

You name the tune. We'll sing
Of anything beneath the sun.
Or moon. We'll tattletale
All secrets but our names.

John, John, do you recognize
My voice?
I feel like I have spent my life
Hanging on.

Timer

for George Lonesome

Hello, I am expired again
For want of a silver dime.

In Iowa City once
The local junkie, Lonesome,
Leaning on a meter, said, Man,
It's all
When the time runs out.

It did. His last letter
From the institution asked
Money to publish
His numerical analysis
Of History.

George, I still count syllables.
My moment, too, is almost up.
The centers of our downtowns scream

Red Flag! Red Flag!

Violations abound. Stay
Mad. I will buy,
And think of you,
A cherry Cadillac, park
Anywhere I want.

Vitamin

Mr. J. C. (53) of Damascus, Arkansas,
Had an enlarged heart, bad valves, poor
Circulation before taking vitamin E.

He reports: "The heart size is reduced,
My circulation and breathing are better
And I have less fainting and few leg cramps."

All that we are happy to know, although
The better off will smile and turn the page,
The worse will be jealous at your improvement.

And though I can see you holding your calf
While the tears pour down until you fall
On the worn carpet in the front room of your house,
My poem is not looking for clear image or moral.

Enough that you never know I write of my heart
That each year it seems both larger and weaker
And therefore my circulation is poorer
For no remedy helps me to get around.

Three Around the Young Gentleman

Way Out on the Way Out
for John Berryman

You must think I'm blind
You push your words in
Till my hands turn red from the wringing
Knuckles all cracked

In fact

My future swells from your grip
Life line slap like a whip
Touch deafen numb and tear

Assur ed
When you join the dead
Body will twitch till the sun set

And mine will too mon brer

Ends

for John Berryman

"*Zany enlivens.*"

Well so. If one palavers past
The grave, I
Can talk to you done John.
Figure you under water.
You always wanted to get to what
Scrawled the skin on the scrotum, ah, us,
Inflected and gendered, oh,
Well so, the day I heard you
Suicided, I felt like
John Berryman.
Another John dead dog gone on,
How
Does every dear John oh God go
Sass
In nation?

Three Around the Young Gentleman

On Falling
for John Berryman

The winds are old, have all
Been breathed by someone,
Sung by a few. I, too,
Laid myself out on the air,
Felt not me fall,
But the great ground rush up,

Big mother kiss, big
Belly whopper.

Every poem, John, is jus
Playing for Time.

What's Mine

My cat makes me laugh.
We are in the dark together,
See, and I say to him,
You are bad as Robert Frost,
Yowling about fences. You are.

Suppose the blue Maltese
Does cross each night
Yard to yard, hedging along,
Belly on the earth, maybe
It's only a shortcut home
To his own bowl of fish,
His own kitchen heaven.

I should buy the place
Next door, I suppose?
Put up a sign keeping out
All cats of a differing stripe?

Let live, I shout from the pool.
And how many times have I told you,
Don't claw the screen!

For a Friend with Two Years to Live

She walks in a world where everything is known.
And as if the colors in her clothes were braille,
Her fingers fret the textures.

Now she tells us of a climb
Upon a ridge not far from here,
The cold rock seeping through her skirt
As she picked her sweater free from burrs.

Alerted to the lightest touch,
Our fingers prickle feeling how
We pluck to keep our own warmth pure.

And so her listeners begin the climb.
We breathe a bit more heavily. We sit.
And we can almost feel our eyes
Tear from the chilly wind.

Heartwood

You chopped the tree down though it held my house
And tore away the brush and cleared a court.
Too young to play, I loved to watch the sport,
So if it cost my house I felt no loss.

From a rickety ladder at net height
The ball was like my globe at school, but white.
I didn't know the rules. It was my game
To see who kept the ball longest in air,
Patting my leather world with his strong hands.
But when it stayed so long I thought it tame,
Someone would slip and miss it bouncing, or
Somebody near the net would thump it down.

Then the turtle came. And volleyball
Raised no more dust in air than catching him.
Two feet across, at least six inches tall,
He eyed the ring of feet, looked for a place to swim,
And finding none, pulled in his legs and tail.
The head stayed part way out. His leather back
Was brown, but stitched and round like half the ball.

"Ride 'im, Romey!" And for a little while
You, father, stood astride half of my globe,
Taller than everyone. O, what a smile!

"There is a story that if you set flame
Beneath a turtle's belly he will crawl
Out of his shell," one of the big men said.
"I wonder if he would?" "Can't ever tell!"

You carried oily rags from the garage
And rolled the turtle on them with a stick
And once it was begun the test was quick.
A match was struck, and caught in seas of fire
The turtle tried to dig down to his mud.

Whoever told the story was a liar.

A summer of scrapes, and bitter bruises, too.
Always your voice to flinch me, "You won't die!"

So I did all a boy can ever do.
I ran away from laughing gods to cry.

It was a wicked summer I recall.
More than a turtle died within his shell
The day house tree and legend fell.

Leavings

It stuns like being present
At the massacre of myself
To turn so at the doorway
And see sprawled on the sofa
My mangled twisted clothing.

Crucified in woolen,
My bent and crippled arms
Torture all composure
And there my severed ankles
Rest in separate leathers.

The vision forces thought
To tear from a frightened past
Red seconds in a war
When all were scattered silly
And frozen in odd forms.

And then to nearer losses,
A first wife and father,
Vanished now for years,
And how I feel the traces
In their personal effects.

I pick up this silk tie
Much as a lover might,
Upon discovering absence,
And hold it to my cheek
To cool the bloody skin.

For fondling these close things
Is tenderness making believe
That I have truly gone
And now that I have known
This night,
      I truly have.

Shorelines

Root of my hair,
Oasis,

I can feel the bottom of you,
Wet with shade.

Nail of my hand, your
Mandarin flick, your
Grub for worms.

Was I the only child
To lift my father's delicate cold
Fearsome eyelid

And look at the nothing
Behind me

And the nothing ahead?

Root of my life,
Atom,
Founding vibration,
What have you washed up?

Folklore

Invariably I look back for help.
In one of my early poems a man
With the world on his hands stands
On the back of a huge turtle.

Those Greeks could tell a myth.
Today I learned the Turkish earth
Is held on the horns of an ox.
Earthquakes when his head shakes.

What story shall we tell
Our children born in our Hell?
Something is obviously shaking
Its head. Some back is breaking.

The Dystrophy of Certain Muscles

It is usually without warning
Just when we have our guard down
So this morning
While we were dreaming
In fragrant lathers, crisp neckerchieves,
Towels steaming,

Into the glare of mirrors they wheeled you,
Everyone more than ordinarily fussy,
And from a mechanical chair
Lifted you and arranged you
In a mechanical chair.
Then they adjusted it.

Grotesque ideas were born:
What style could you possibly wish?
Would they hold up a mirror and ask
Do you approve?

Or would they take a crazy glass
To make you see your form
Straight as a razor,
Tall as a barber,
Smooth as a Lucky Tiger.

We could all bolt upright,
Stagger outside like bloody Caesars
Crying ruin, weeping betrayal.
Unpinned,
We could fall apart at the seams.

But the scissors
Snicker.
Our hair gets thinned.
The ritual keeps us disciplined.

Friendly Game

So. You're blind. Well, that's the way with war.
No man comes back the one he was before.
As you come tapping toward me on the street,
My mind feels back to where the boys would meet.

Up went the hoop behind O'Neill's garage
And soon the grass was scuffed and dribbled from
A round bare spot of ground where boys could dodge
Their suppers to play basketball. And come
The time of choosing up, the first pick took
You always on his team. You were the best
For neighborhoods around, and wore a look
That said your play with us was half in jest.

You scorned backboards. The idea was to win
With handicap, agility and grin.
Rebounds fell into your hands. The sets
You threw wore out imaginary nets,
And we heard future coliseums roar
As those shots fell to swell the final score.
A lot of guys just played to get a tan.
Why did I always face you for my man?

Has no one ever noticed your slight smile,
As if you heard a cheering from the past?
As you go by, my hand, in the old style,
Twitches a shot. I fake you out at last.

Monarch

It fluttered in the fallen leaves.
The cat put out one paw to bring
Up a butterfly with a torn wing.

Tom had one hind leg crippled
When he was young and fought.
I can imagine what he thought.

Fairbanks, Alaska

The white house belongs to Leo Hardy.
Eight years ago his wife gassed herself.
The fact that it was a Florence Range
Stuck in the family memory
For no reason.

The two sons married and had girls.
And when the older, Martin, was twenty-nine,
He went out to the dark garage
And stuffed its broken windows.
Then he started the engine of his car.

Above the mailbox that reads Leo Hardy,
Above the long back stairsteps of the white house,
Windbells hang,
Though, in the Interior, wind is rare.

Today the black crows are soaring
Near the white house
And the glass bells make clear notes
That carry.

Louise Is from Iowa

She is plain.
And natural.
And her forehead is fair.
Through the grain of her hair
One can hear the midwest rustle.
That is not important today, for

This last year she has taken to laughing
With a slight reservation of breath,
The first nuance of an autumn.
And the fur on my bones rustles.

Rarely, but more often, and now,
She looks up at me like an earth
I have bladed part of my life upon.
And her eyes are brown open wounds.

So Lonely in Hartford

for Wallace Stevens

Well Wallace, there is me and you now.
And that glass of water.

Bet you thought no one would find you,
Bet you paid premiums.

Maybe even guessed
Someone would add booze
Or get seasick one.

Not though do a figure eight near the brim.
Tip his tam to ya goin past on one foot.

Or sit on the safedge, cast a mean fly,
Bring a girl down to be alone.

Bet you thought it was your pool.
Put up a po em to keep out the riff raff.

Well Wallace,
Never forgive you Wallace,
So lonely in Hartford,
And how you had to spell it out near the end.

Children's Verse
for Debra Segal

She is coming toward me on wooden legs
All right
Is Debra

Exactly as explained in the pathetic newspapers
Iterated in black and white nitrate

Forget the poetry
Each of my practiced feelings is a failure
She looks up out of a crippled vision
Scarcely under control

Oh

Behind her twisted smile
Thousands of manhours of motherlove
And fatherfear

Staggering steps

Debra crutches toward us past the delicate china
Past . . .
And the expensive furniture rugs tapestries
Turn to a linen lace
The air is scented with concern
Debra is

We hold our breaths afraid to even
Smell perhaps each others fright
What are the others thinking
Debra is walking

Fear of all the bad dreams now

Debra is stepping smiling toward us

In our living room

Whose reach exceeds yes her
Frightening so trustful

Librarian

Yes yes she knew it.
Here even,
In the thinnest of positions,
Where only competence was required,

Error has multiplied.
Surface has been flawed
Like a bitten yellow pencil
Used only to express
Nerves.

She pats a stray dry curl
And another ravels from its clip.
Glasses dangle at the end of their chain
As she rubs the bridge of her nose.

The library is quiet.
Very quiet.
Tomorrow she will pick up her check
With exactly that silence.

Behind her
The books sing and sing.

Artistic

He could hear music blow
Toward and away,
Waver right and left.

No wonder
Dogs barked.

He saw paintings as heavy
Or light.
Imagined the hairs drag in the pigment,
Palette knife plaster the canvas
No wonder
Friends laughed.

One day he hung himself up
For all to view.

Only Eyes

Rainy day driving
And the wiperbeat wiperbeat wiperbeat

Fancies of a wife dead
And another girl other girl

And a daughter dead and a mother
Other no other no other

Watchout wiperbeat lonely eyes

Specialty

Glottochronology is my favorite
Science, though you'd never heard
About it. Men trained in this
Study how words distort as time
Passes, how the tongue muscles
Itself, how the bones change
As a result of meaning shifting,

How the face finally expresses.

It would seem evolution favors
More and more communication
And very slowly and I mean
Very slowly all of us poets
Are having a visible impact.

I am half in love with
Iambic pentameter myself
Because I like the way tongues
Flap flap. Something sensual
There. But I can do
Without it. And sometimes

Without how your lips got that way.

Advertising

The front of your brain is blue.
Green in some lights.
Back of that, I am told,
All is grey.
And is so for everyone.

Which should do to make suspect
All who claim colorful
Dreams, schemes, personalities,
Anything made of idea.

You. Keep up the good front.

Likeness

The birds on those telephone wires
Perch like notes on a staff.
They bear an obvious resemblance,
But at this moment are quiet as a book.

My wife often takes out her music
And soon little birds punctuate the air.
I hear each typewriter key from another,
Though I admit deeper strains fill my head.

What if everything we saw came together
And the surf of the clouds and the wave
Ran off the wet page of the maestro
And he couldn't continue for his tears?

Flying Circus

On the road the dry leaves clown.
Summer's blue tarpaulin's down.
Frost has slackened the pennant vines
And struck the scarlet climber's lines.
Meadow-wide, the spendthrift trees
Have frittered away their currencies.

The last act of a summer run
Plays to a standing house of one:
Barnstorming butterflies sweep past;
A cricket band in the brush has massed;
Locusts sway on their stems with grace;
A spider sets her net. In case.

Seasoned performers, I catch breath
At this cool disregard of death,
And though, aloof, you never pause,
Acknowledging my brisk applause,
I number in your staunch supporters.
Daredevils, where are your winter quarters?

—1958

A Dark Outline

The dentist held up those odd shadows
So that over the years
I could see how things were going.

My hand for example shad*ed* this page.
ed stuck out under the index finger.
Thanks yet none of the bones were showing.

Nails manicured in Miami,
Palm discovered in Alaska,
Sperm walking San Francisco.

Soon I will go into the globe in a slow flowing,
Leaving only this poem glowing.

Pro Vita Sua

Having summarized my bio,
I am now writing a poem
On the backside of a life
Typed full of errors.

Two sorts of summary show through.

My feelings are probably on edge like this
Page catches the purposeless breeze.

If I could,
I would
Slide out on the first wind.

I will, instead,
Try to sit still.

Hold myself up to the light like this.

A Needle's Eye

You'd think the children would believe,
But they have ever thought untrue
Stories that include 'do not.'
They are the least listened to.

I like to think those widened eyes
Are opened to admit a world,
But little wisdom always doubts
The truth in which it will be whirled.

My grandson grows incredulous
At my belief in darning flies:
That needles will knit up his lips
And stitch his lids down on his eyes.

I hate to think these simple tales
Are only true in adult lands,
That these fine threads are only felt
In tighter times, by older hands.

—1958

Central System

Everyone please note the frog
Like last week's dog
Is vertebrate
Is whole of spine
Is not yet dead

So naught will interfere
With the experiment
We amputate his brain
By the simple expedient
Of cutting off his head

There

Now hanging him from wire and fish hook
We take a bit of acid dipped white gauze
Apply it to his back
Note that in your note book without a pause
His hind leg reaches up to rub away
What he has never known since he was spawned
Beneath a log
In a green lily pond

Which proves the spine of any headless frog
Thus touched with sulphur brine
Though any acid serves
Connects directly to the

Nerves

To a Beauty

That ugly girl, who seated by the wall,
Watches you moving at my side,
Has a better touch for distance,
Knowing your beauty through her pride.

Ignorant, you have been visited,
Toured like the rich palace of a king
Who never noticed, even as a child,
What could make some marveling peasant sing.

Resort

Every summer they came,
Clapboard shingle and gull.
Wouldn't miss him,
Blind at the piano,
Still magic moving magic.

Husband died first she
Came twice after that.
Once soon after.
Once much later.
Years in between,
Clapboard shingle and gull,

And then there were none.

Tongues

Louis Tuleja could spit thick
Gobs of phlegm further
Than anyone in the gym
And with an aim so fine
He'd blot the brassy doorknob
Your *were* about to turn

Or hang one from the ceiling
Right over your head
And you would cringe like Damocles
Calculating tensile strength
Or tonsil strength maybe

And Kookie Braniff's shoeshine shop
Had all its smokey windows
Stuffed with old green poolhall felt
To smother down
The drafts and weathers

He'd lounge mornings away
In his palace of dead air
Huffing great mouthfuls slowly till
They settled over the fingers
Of dull black coathooks or the toes
Of upturned iron footrests

In those days a poet swore
His mouthings would be stable
On the page and in the mind
But age has blown him back to find
In cloudy word and line
This small personal triumph
Of a kind

Creative Writing Notebook: Lesson No. 1

Byron had a club foot.
He made love to his sister anyhow.
She was very beautiful
With many admirers.
She picked the brother with the club foot.

It is called swimming the Hellespont.

Milton liked the look of a king's head.
Off the body.
When in came the new king, he took a royal
Long look at Milton.
Milton stared back blindly.

It is called swimming the Hellespont.

Poets prove freedom by living it daily.
It is called swimming the Hellespont.
Anyone who can swim can be a poet.

Melodramatics

I

Curtains
Says the villain

Spotting consequence
Trammeling down the tracks

Foiled again

For heroes kisses
Thrown flowers
Champagnes
Big Party
Up at the armory

While shivering in his cape
Waiting the last freight
Out of this crummy town

Curtains
Says the villain
I simply tried to teach them

Style

II

Foiled
Does that mean

No more locomotives
No more hemp

Shall I do pushups
Get me a tan
Practice an open smile
A glad hand
Find a job
Work uptoit slow

After all
Nobody even looked at her

Never thought of her

That way

Was always Sis

Before

III

What is a poorboy to do
Other side of the tracks boy

Was it the threats?

But when she finds
It must be violent

What then Trueblood?

When she finds
I merely act your boyhood dreams

When she sees me
In your embarassed eyes

Admits to herself
She wanted me so many times

In the black of night

IV

There will be another time girl
Daddy finally gone

All of it yours at last
Far as you can see

There will be another time
By my filthiest oath

(*$&!*)__ (+&=) /%$¢

I will lift your life from

Those frail hands

The Prom: Three Poems

The Queen

Bats her eyes,
Flashes her green lids, she is
Drunk enough not to hope any longer
Others have drunk enough not to notice
She is taller than her partner.

Her bobbed hair bobs upon her bare shoulders.
It should be cut a bit but it grows so fast.
One can hardly keep up anymore.

The music is faster and her partner puffs.
He is also sweating, how does one say, profusely?
Her eyes shine again greeny like fireflies.

Is there no sweet black bird in the dark
To sight to soar to dip to take in beak
Her downy neck?

She would be Leda to a bat,
This poor Cleopatra,
Too tall for any serious love
And terrified of snakes.

Wallflower

What do they know, pretty and perfumed?
What if she can't dance, the boys wink anyway.

And later on when they are all tucked in
With teddybears and sugarplums and mother
Wets their forehead and turns out the light,
When the boys are at the diner drinking coffee,
Afraid to be the first one to go home,

She'll roll the blankets under from the right
And roll the blankets under from the left
And when she is cocooned up tight,
Warm as any butterfly,
She'll reach one tender finger down
And dance with all the handsome boys in town.

The Prom: Three Poems

Chaperone

The crinoline outmodes him.
If he could
He'd stop the band, round up the girls,
Gather all the pinkness home.

Instead he drifts,
His hands remembering starch.

Why pick on him each dance?
He wears a bow tie and he smokes a pipe,
Is easy with the girls and jokes the boys.

He wishes that he would go bald,
Get paunchy, testy, be a principal.

He reaches all the way across the gym
To pull a junior's bodice higher.
Then he pulls it down again,
Kisses the nipples of her breasts,
Tears her underthings to shreds.
They couldn't stop him till he raped
Maybe even three.

He rubs his pipe against his nose
And the oil makes the grain come out.
His wife is knitting.
She looks up at him and smiles.

Moon Poems

Projection

A bright moon can bring down the sky.
Tonight there is a bright moon, I
Have been brought down. Dark and low
Falls a foreshortened dim shadow.

If blackness has its shapes, those shapes
Are absences. But this one apes
My posture, queries all I've phrased
From life. I'm questioned. And I'm phased.

Wan and in eclipse, I mock
The moon back, and begin to talk
Of differences face to face.
Moon men are a crusty race.

I quiz him how his fires died.
His craters argue that he tried.
Though guessing that he's deep and gold,
I kid about his hidden cold.

He asks me of my darker side.
I throw him shadows, and my hide
Obscures a more complete display.
I press him why he pales at day.

We'll be both finally found out,
Discovered down to the last doubt.
They'll learn his scars are spread the same
Over both sides. Though who's to blame?

And as for me, they'll learn that all
I would or could tell them, was all.
They won't believe one pockmarked page.
They'll say I lied about my Age.

—1962

The Tracks of Tyros

With nothing more important up
Seven of us meet to spin
One Saturday afternoon away,
Guests of the government.

Somewhere in an atmosphere
Turned deep blue by the yellow sun,
A tiny eye at incredible speed
Watches our weathers.
Technicians perk their huge
Aluminum ears and wait.

They warm their brains up
And they wait. The time will tell.
The time will tell these circuits
When to think. They are searching
Our heavens.

We want to know what's up,
What's for us in the next few days:
Omens spelled out on a plastic strip
(which stretches under too much strain).

We stand a little space apart
One of the machines is red
And someone asks it for a Coke.
It doesn't laugh; it goes
About its father's business, scanning stars.

And we are told that in the future
(which is very near)
This system will be totally unmanned.
The machines become excited.
The bird is overhead and squawks
Its message, and a miracle
Faithful to the hour
Shines to perfection. For a moment
We see ourselves
A moving map, a present globe.

Moon Poems

Privileged, we peer at coasts
And clouds, we ponder boundaries,
We meditate from a point of view
A thousand statute miles from dizziness.

And then the little moon has set.
We pull on coats and fumble for our keys,
Ignite our cars and spin away
Over the same geographies
That we could not decipher minutes past.

The tracking station leaves our mirrors
Which only show the way we had arrived.

—1962

Moon Flight

Launch

He will become excited.
Within certain limits.
Then the elements will fume.

And with technicians numbering seconds
Like lovers
In some long drawn ponderous good-bye,
He will enter a silent heavy hesitance,
And then the timelessness of travel.

Some will turn away, others
Will follow him out of mind,
And a few will think, another

Emissary against dragons.

The Sea of Frigidity

Light, clumsy, breath
Coming upon demand,
He will stand
Upon the history
Of a million, upturned, night-torn eyes.

He will pick up a pebble of the moon.
It will be like the end of any love,
And he will stand,
Encratered, desolate,
Upon the stiffened shores of meteors,
The sharp horizon abruptly
Near, and a clouded future
Pendant in his sky.

Terminal

The thunder on the moon is silent.
It is no less there. Ask
Any of the moon's pedestrians.
He will smile the smile of

No one *you* know.
And then his lids will rise,
Like the doors on storm cellars,
And you will see emerge
The ancient look of the survivor,
Pupils wide with aftermath,
The mind's streets filled with leaves and litter,
Black homes,

And a snapped blue sparking.

—1963

Blues in Black and White

Down in the Ghetto

Big male chromosome coming down the street
Stop in front of the can dee store
Light his cee gar from the sole of one boot

He see the little girl chromosome
With the red dress on

She say dit dit dit

He say dah dah dah

She say again dit dit dit

Now that is my dominant strain chile
Your recessive too

S O S when I saw how
Hath God wrought you

Welfare Shout

She got high clear plastic heels
And red red lacquer on her toes,
Few blue veins back of her legs.
I love her just the same.

Two false teeth on the right side,
Big brass loop in one ear,
Always stands with one hand on her hip,
I love her just the same.

Brown love line down her belly,
Stretch marks either side,
She done a lot of romance,
I love her just the same.

Please, govermint, send me my check,
Hurry the mailman on.
But even if we both go thirsty,
I love her just the same.

Blues in Black and White

Sharpy

Let me tell you this one thing
Before you go puttin on.

We all end up down and dirty.
You cant fight City Hall.

Beg among the pigeons,
Get you a fine statue,

Comes to the same thing buddy:
Down and dirty down down down

Down and dirty down

Owner

If I could sit here always,
Sun on my face,
Grass stem in my teeth,

Leaning here always,

But theres hay in the meadow,
Storm in the far sky.

If I could sit here always,
Sun on my face.

Dont it always happen dog?
Dont it   always happen.

Understanding Is a Tone of Voice Blues

Our cat is so lazy
He get sore if you make him purr.

Why our cat is so lazy
You can pick him up,
Move him out,

Put him down.
He open one eye,
Tuck his left paw under his chin,
Open both eyes.
My, he say, it all different.

How I get heah?

Now that is lazy, mama.
But thats how
I make
Love.

Pick me up.
Move me out,
Put me down.

How I get heah?

And if you dont understand me,
I say *if* you dont understand me,
Well thats the

Understanding is a Tone of Voice

Blues.

Understanding Is a Tone of Voice Blues Part Two

This is the flip side, brothers.
And sisters.

Said before our cat is lazy.
He fall asleep standin up.
Fall over like a bookend.
Or a doorstop.

Keep him anyway:
Props up books of poems.
Dont eat much,
Keeps the screen door tight,
Flies out.

And that's how
I make
Love:

Keep your door tight mama, hold
Your old book shelf.

How to Pick a Mistress, Or

Cat love the smell of my arm pit.
Nuzzle the nose up there like cat will.

Days I think
Last man on earth
No five day deodorant stick.

Patriotick.
Flags behind me when I walk

And

Thinkin some cat I might meet,
Bathe each and every morning
Like sunwork.

So

If a big angel with a smug smile,
Flat on his back, rubbin his wings
In some big dusty bowl

Can be imagined

Well that's me in my shower.
And this song is the flutter of the wings
On my guardian.

Heavenly. Even earthy,
Dust to dust speakin.

Pickanangelfeatherangelanyfeather,
My COY kitty.

A Writer's Attic

Moving is a kind of dying. One binds fast
As many ends and odds out of the past
As a sense of the ridiculous allows.
Some awkward items are too large, have lost
The magic of compelling an attachment.
The least important things are left for last.

One time sophisticate of the dining room,
That bureau of mahogany veneer,
Warped, and its one eye clouded over,
Used to frighten me with dark designs.
I wonder at its humbling. Mischief
Seems the new limit of imagination
And I can't think it cares for its demotion,
Though more than that is stolen by the years:
Books and clothing I grew out of, toys,
Some games, these could be handed down, although
Letters, photographs, newspaper clippings
Where I won a second or third prize,
I do not want to keep along. Or leave.
I carry bushels of them out as trash,
Mail them, in the fire, to the North Pole,
Which is the only spot I've ever heard
A hope to go to once it's spent in ink.
Or a fear even.

                        Enough of being childish.
A grown man couldn't help but snigger archly
If I let him overhear my musing.
With ease one must incinerate his trifles,
For who would have his pettiness revealed.
I carry bushels of it out as trash.
It is as if my bland objective eye
Won't understand. Or sympathize, perhaps.
I don't completely understand myself,
But at the aftertime of any loss,
There is deserves a pause of mind:
The what to take away, the what to leave behind.

Showing My Age
(1978)

Eddie's Bar

The private secretary giggles behind her hand.
The crippled jeweler projects his
Guffaw.

Something is showing again, some
Crack in the mahogany
Against which we all lean.

If I am sober, even
Laughter is served up
To life's taste.

Haw. All jokes are dirty.

And are on us.

Pruning Roots

Back from vacation, I labor
Cutting the great ficus tree,
Limb from limb. Straight through root
Upon root the chain saw whines, then
Strains under load.

My father brings his seventy-seven
Years to bear. He is satisfied
Digging some in the old leaves,
Being handy man helpful.

The wife's whole family gathered,
Three times in three days,
Plains folk slow to work up
To questions. Tomatoes down there
Good? What is the rain like?
The children gather round
My Cadillac. Get away,
Gramma says, get away.

This last trip I stayed clear
Of the university, saw
No old professors, asked
Questions only of farmers.

My father puts down his mason jar
Full of iced mango and papaya juice
And stands up, ending the break.
I flip my cigarette butt away.
Root sap cakes my sticky hands.

It will be the devil getting off.

Black and White and Color

When my uncle Arty Katt
Took the Luger pistol his brother
Brought back from World War Number Two
And put it into his soft palate
You can imagine the end of the story.

Fired once from his job at Worthy
Paper, he sent for a book
So that he could tell
The top ten men in fine paper
That he had worked his way
From floor sweeper after school
Up to General Manager.
He found out the top man in fine
Was him. He couldn't write
To himself. Number Two was Kodak.

Wise now, he worked and drank
Too much, too much, the relatives
Said to one another, at a distance.

You see, my Uncle Arty
Made the stiff fine paper
Behind your every silly photo.
He made you all stand up
And become a kind of History.
Well, unfortunately for him,
He knew it.

Torsion

When I was ten my father
Bought an old blue Chevy
To drive to Ludlow
And visit my mother's mother,
A big fat lady with warmth
Like her cast iron oven.
We'd go by way of Indian Bend.

The frame of the Chevy was twisted
And so if my father drove
Too fast around the long curve the two
Doors would fly open.

Years of cars have passed
And years of travel. The family
Retired from Massachusetts
Down A1A to Florida.

Over that line of palms is the ocean.
Most times we don't think of it,
Except some nights when certain
Flags run up on the yachts. Then
We know the sea is gathering and
Leaping. The wind picks up.

Under enough pressure, we know
The doors of our lives would spring open.

Cartwheels

Old man Sydlo delivered bread
One horse cart with rubber wheels
Whip like a flag, collar on the horse,
Old man Sydlo delivered bread

Chrapek's Pontiac Reed's Garage
Lincoln Park and Saturday softball
Tennis courts flooded and frozen for hockey
Lincoln Grove and MacArthur Circle

Poolhall Friday Nick the Greek
Bowling candlepins, snow on the roof
Old man Sydlo delivered bread
Chicopee High School rah rah rah

Foils

Taught fencing as a boy,
I learned the short lunge and the far,
The parry, and the feint.
The Frenchman I called only "Master"
Seemed to know but the English word "Again!"

The world has differed little from
That long black mat and heavy arm.

Sometimes I stand and face my man
Dressed in a business suit and patent shoes,
Upon a Turkish carpet thick with design,

Relaxed, smiling,

Tips kept up in each other's eyes.

Over the Gulf

It is July in Seventy-Seven.
The Captain informs us in two languages,
Cuba is under the left wing.
I do not inform anyone
It is the anniversary of The Bomb.

Foreigners, you whose wet tongues
Shape secret meanings, whose
Hands fill the air with intimations,
Whose eyebrows ¿question?
Or are making some easy statement,

Be ready to regard me, handsome
American, rich in leather luggage,
Dozing past Communism. Money
Is only my current medium of exchange.

Talk

One must consider, my dear, the dollar
Stands well against the peso at this moment.
I do recall the franc before the war,
And the Taxco silver, though impure
And common, might be considered.
Camino Real is the only place to stay.
Tennis on the roof, you know.
I cannot personally abide the food
But Fouquet's service, well,
At least as good as Old Miami.
Don't buy the clothes. Oh my,
You have so much to look forward to.
I can't say I will ever go again.
Though the hats. And the dark men in the plaza.

Organization of American States

The Mason-Dixon Line has moved
Down to divide Panama with a canal.
The deputies of two hemispheres
Gather under the moon over Miami.

Si, say the potential rebels,
Smiling beneath black mustaches.
They have oily skins and export raw
Materials. When they ask about
The Yankee dollah, we tell'm.

They carry the same look in the eye
As their father Indians who drifted
Down from Mongolia across the tundra,
Spearing bison en route.

Under the great Southern Cross
They have kept better time
Than any civilization.
They know how to wait, and watch
The North Americano Big Board.
When a crack appears here and there,
They mutter behind their hands.

Peasants are like dandelions.
They seed. And will not stay
Off the lawns.

Spider

It came across the green rug frighteningly
Quick as a hyphen, slap
Slap, I struck it, newspaper
Newspaper. The legs folded up
Like the spines of an umbrella
And I sat back breathing harder
Than that small exertion.

Something had crept into my breath.
Some gossamer constriction.

Kill a large beast with a gun.
Even a man shoot down.
But the spider does not ever die, darts

Back when you least expect.

Inside Knowledge

Come friend
Come

Stand up in your pentangled black wings

And make a deal

I had not truly expected
And so was completely unready

When he stood up and unfolded
Inside me

I thought you would come from without
I said

I never do
He said

Jack Smith, Magician

Look, no top hat. Look, no cane.
Sure they must be there,
We stare. We wonder

What alias he will go by next.
Jack Smith. You can't fool us
Forever, but

We must admit
We *are* perplexed:

How does he do those people tricks?
That common name as well,
Jack Smith.

Lawyer? Liar? Legislator
From some hidden land?
No one sees him lift a hand.

Oh, we give up!
Oh, tell us how!

Jack Smith says that's
Enough for now.

And takes one long (invisible) bow.

Forty Four

Divisible now by two, four and eleven,
I am three quarters of the way to heaven.

Next year if I am still alive,
I am most certain to divide by five.

So let me stop (for sixty will be plenty)
To be replaced by three bright men of twenty.

Runner

Dad ran rum
Over the border.

They strapped tin
To the black Buick,

Came across at Laconia.
Then he married
A redhead and had me.

Mother settled that
Wild Canuck into
A plant supervisor.

He leans way back now
In the striped Florida
Lawn chair and says,

Life, she's only give
For a short while.

Peripatetic

The countdown was perfect. We
Clinked champagne as the torch rose
And came up to us from the land.
Our jet banked and angled then, and
Yes, we had timed everything right.
It flew directly by our windows till,
Over our heads, we watched
The bright burst of staging.
They were off for the moon.

We were off for Tallahassee,
To talk, to drink, to meet
The Secretary of the State of Florida.
The Captain came back on the air
To hope we had enjoyed the flight,
Especially the view of Saturn.

The hatch opened. We stepped
Gingerly down aluminum stairs
Under a blazing sun into the strange
Architecture of a sleepy village.
Our feet seemed slow and heavy. Speech
Slurred on the hot air. The sand
Was reddish. The trees were hung
With the beards of mosses. Where
Was this place?

We lugged the clumsy baggage
Of our brief suvival, hopped
Into the ground transportation,
Listened to news of local interest.
The native driver smiled,
Where you boys from?

We did get home. We are
Splashed down upon Miami Beach.
All travel is the same, all
Destination and arrival. No one
Goes anywhere. Simple as Einstein,
The time goes by.

Doctor of Medicine

We meet at Xanadu of Florida
Where his mustache was colored.
His face is flushed from the chemicals
And we walk to a dark bar
To talk while his skin cools.

His wife is leaving him.
Janov again. Not bad enough
His patients, now his wife
Has shouted *her* doctor says
He must join her in the primal
Screaming, lay himself
Open to the cries of birth.
Crap, he says to the air, crap!
The bar is full of painted ladies.
We leave after a few drinks.

He has given up his El Dorado.
The Coupe de Ville is more
Reliable, you understand, doesn't
Need so much attention, the El
Was always under overhaul.

She gets the house naturally,
And the kids and bank account.
He is presently in the apartment
Behind the clinic. More
Than a year he's been there.

She knows nothing about his art,
And, for Christ's sake, don't
Tell her. Your're the *only*
One he's trusted to have a look.
Even his nurses never enter.

Four keys for the back doors.
Been robbed over and over,
For the drugs, you know, and
Can you imagine? They never
Steal the paintings from the walls,
Allthough nothing of real value

Graces the clinic. Good,
But not anything like what
He keeps in the apartment,
Never mind in the vault.

Fourth in his class at Lehigh.
And a failure. They quote
His classmates, and he answers,
Yes, I helped him through
Anatomy. But here, he says,
Lighting the room, gesturing
With his whole arm at the
Dazzling art, is kept success.

I take a deep breath and hold
It. A dozen yard-square paintings,
All portraits, all people sitting
To have their essence fingered
By the great assessors. Held
Forever in the carved wood
Gilded frozen surf of the frames.

A waiting room full of faces.
My eyes look into their eyes
For their inner pangs. There,
Of all of them, on the left,
The soul of a peasant overflows
The pigments of his aging face.
Van Gogh. Original. Van Gogh.

Here, he says, is a Caravaggio,
Though Erich Schlier calls it
Mario Pretti, making it worth
Hundred of thousands less.
Fool, he adds, I ought to know,
Doing my own x-rays of the inner
Structure. No one believes his eyes,
Anymore, and seeks deeper proof.

I stare into the eyes of Mather Brown's
Martha Washington. Hard, political

Eyes. They seem to know precisely
How history will find her. She
Looks out knowing everything.
And the pain is there. I ask myself,
Is this the doctor's heart?
Or subject's? artist's? mine?
I let my breath out in a sigh.

Tomorrow a midwest museum
Will decide five hundred thousand
For nineteen out of his collection.
He is extremely hopeful. And
A little nervous. You understand.

I stagger from the clinic,
Mumbling a complex good-bye:
A few words soothing the divorce,
My hopes the purchase
Goes his way, my compliments
To his full-time restorer
Who has evidently handled
Time's disguises expertly.
Yes, they do look pristine,
Even the facial cracking natural.

Twenty years of tracking down
The sources of creation, and now,
Somehow, he's ready to sell off
The whole collection, the whole
Vault even, somehow. After
Those long years the population
Of his inner life can go. He
Is ready to give up everybody.

I say good night. On the way
To my home, those faces glow
Brighter than headlights.
I am only his poor patient.
With a case of serious nerves.
He will see me again next week.

I sit for an original.
Will he come through my
Lettering? Will they? Will I
Show through? Will all of us
Gather in some large beating
Beating heart? It behooves
Everyone to get some rest.

Storages

There is no one in the library,
And I only wander, looking for nothing
Especially. The books sleep on the shelves
Of the black stacks, centuries thinking
In their various styles. Bound. Ordered.
In Reserve. And I remember

Waking to a night full of dream, once,
And I propped myself up in the dark barracks.
Men tossed and talked and noised and here
And there an arm or leg was thrown from
Under the drab covers. Tomorrow
Two thousand men would hit the silk
At once. The North Carolina dawn
Would fill with men clutching at air
And the added dangers of each other.

Dreams say what if as well as a poem.

Something stirs in my old memories:
One early morning I came upon a zoo
Tiger. I stood stock still, and then
A dream's weight shook her terrible paw.

Florida versus Zamora

Beyond all reasonable doubt,
One can hear this case open
And shut. The eighty year old lady,
The fifteen year old robber killer,
The spending spree at Disney World,
Defense attorney with grey temples,
Mickey Mouse and Donald Duck,
The sober judge, young prosecutors,
The Electric Light Parade.

And, of course it is a First,
A trial on trial on television.
We watch in comfort from our easy chairs.

Defense says television made him do it:
Exposure to the nightly violence pulled
The trigger, call as witness
The famous actor of detective parts, call
Writers, advertisers, experts on effects, call
No, the judge will not allow,
The prosecutors do objects,
Irrelevant, irrelevant, irrelevant,
Sustained.

It is evident the boy is not insane.
It is evident that television is not sane.
It is evident the judge is not insane.
It is not evident society is sane.

They never find the gun. The jury
Sends a message to the judge:
Will his honor let it see itself?

But Ronnie has his short life's wish.
He is a lady killer on teevee, star
In a drama of his own. He is impassive.
And beyond all reasonable doubt,
His face is cold as a glass screen.

After a fair and full deliberation
On this blank day of October,

Charges the judge. We find,
Answers the black and white jury of his peers,

Ronnie (medical certainty)
Albert (diminished capacity)
Zamora (conditioned reflex)
Guilty in the First Degree.

Nothing flickers in Zamora's color.
He has won a million replays.

True to the judge's vow,
The burden fell upon the State,
Television has outlived the trial.
And once again, we have been entertained.

Poll the jury. Guilty. So say we all.

The Final Days

Turning the last page, closing
The book, wondering where in God's name
To enter it on the stained shelves
In my library devoted mostly to poetry,
I sat quietly for a long time
In the certain knowledge for the first time
I could not be the President.

It is not corruption, I
Could be that corrupt, not
The endless parade of dignitaries.
I could rise to statemanship.

It is, very much, the adherence:
The urgent concern with civilization.

Some years ago, in Chicago I think,
I read my poems at the city college
And after, went with friends to lunch
At a private club on the fiftieth floor
Which they were very proud of.
Prudential. That building.

And I looked out at the great new
Sky scraper going up for U.S. Steel,
Sheathed in marble to show strength
And the hard opulence of power.

And the brave workers building it
Had painted fourstory giant
Initials of their girl friends,
For the whole city to see for months
Till the sheath rose to cover
And entomb them. They would last,
Invisible, testifying forever
To the strange human wish
To last. Only that. To last.

I look, often, at English,
Staring past words, past the odd
Shapes of our letters, our queer

Attempt to catch and hold the fast
Brain's grasping blur. Perhaps
I become more atavistic
With the years' disclosure, but

Always my knowledge is with me.
Knowing the entropy of the great
Burning gaseous stars, and the unfathomed
World under the sea, and in the sea,
And indeed in the drop of the sea.

I have looked through the telescope
With bare retina, holding the breath.
I have looked through the microscope
With bare retina, holding the breath.

It is, very much, the adherence,
The attempt to impress one's meaning
Forever on the current of Time.
I could not be the President.

Nixon, nix, no, nag, new, Agnew,
Nix new, new nag, no no. Put
Your name name on the moon, put
Your colors on the bunting,
Agree on a flag and fly it.
Speak yourselves hoarse.

Kick at the wind.
Shout back at the sea.

I am weary from this book.
Characters less intelligent
Than an average novel,
More cunning, involved in plot,
Each held in his little truth.
There is too much verisimilitude.
I am sick of their names.

Put them under.

Put them under stone.

Calendar

The Administrator of the Arts
Waits for his lawyer to arrive
For tennis, as usual an hour late
And even at that, it looks like rain.

There is a poetry festival tomorrow.
He will do the introductions,
Careful as always about pedigree
And subtle with puffery. Ah,
There are accounts to do in the mean-
Time, on the corporation he is
Forming to standardize forms.

Once again, the marketing man
Is not returning calls, a break-
Down in communications. He will
Take the s o b over the coals
In a future where he will least
Expect it. A university president
Calls and they talk about money.
Nothing is resolved, but promises
Are made. Most things will never
Eventuate anyway. His secretary
Has been, all week, sick. He
Worries about catching cold
On the eve. On the eve of . . .

It is always on the eve of.
Nothing in any business is ever
Over. Christ, he remembers
He forgot to get new tennis
Balls. Also he is out of postage
Stamps. And new rejection slips
For the magazine he edits must
Be printed up. And new letterhead.
It is increasingly obvious
He is running

Behind.

The Inner Ear

The black yellow cab driver stopped
Before the Nashville Hyatt Regency.
I was slated a participant in

The Official Conference on Humanity.
Will wonders never. In the plane
A black fly crossed my path.
Omens should get themselves straight.
What can you believe nowadays?

Up in the clear plastic elevator
To the fourteenth floor. I had found
Justice. My inner ear began a slow
Ache. Pressures. I sat down with
Specialists in values from ten states.
The pitcher broke out in a cold sweat.

Lately mostly I've been reading lives.
Luciano, Daley, Kennedy versus Nixon,
And the lifeless lives of corporations,
Banks, and agencies. Character
Is fate. Oh, FBI. Oh, CIA.
America comes down to guns and money.

The Justice Panel starts its deep
Discussion. Do we mean social
Justice? Or shall we broaden talk
This once, investigating definition?
The lawyers quickly form a block.
Let's keep it in the courts, where they
Feel comfortable, for instance, should
A judge be appointed or elected.
The U.S. Senator says, elected, by
All means. The bank directors murmur,
No, appointed. The professors turn
Their pages absently. The Chairman
Moves us to another subject: poverty.

I shall jump up on the table shouting,
We are all equally impoverished. God

And Shakespeare both agree. But I
Sit still, remembering Justice Shallow.
The morning drones not even on.
The fat black man named Lincoln falls
Asleep. The members move, the chairman
Notes, nothing is going anywhere.
A chilly puddle forms under the pitcher.

At lunch I thank and thank and butter up
My bread. The steak is under par.
She's Chairman of the League of this.
He's Director of the Group for that.
What panel are you on? I'm Work.
I'm Health. I'm Politics. I'm
Getting dizzy from my inner ear.

The afternoon convenes. Right where
The morning left us off. Apologies
To the chairman: I suffer. He hopes
I will be able to continue. I
Hope so along with him, but.

That night I miss the riverboat
Banquet. And suddenly I close
My suitcase upon everything
And check my reservations. Yes,
They are firm. And First Class.

In the morning I rise above
The low clouds gripping Nashville.
Blind to me, I'm sure, Justice
Resumes its adversary pattern.
Tomorrow they will resolve. I
Will go to the beach, pick up a shell,
Hold it tight to my inner ear
And listen. It will sing the same
Old wordless tune of underwater
Labyrinthine everchanging ways.
I will hear the values of the moon.

Atop the Ford Foundation

From the white linen tablecloth
The view is straight down
On an indoor garden.

The magnolia trees have not
Quite bloomed yet,
Though one can imagine flowers.

In the very center is a square
Pool in which men wishing great favors
Have tossed little coins.

The coins lie on the bottom
Like skeletons of wishes,
Tips of a cheap munificence showing.

My mind comes back to the linen
Where a patient official
Carefully explains his rejection.

I am out on the street again
Before I know it
And a cab pulls up like a shark.

Where to, buddy?
I am at a loss even for words
But I say, The Sheraton.

Lucky for me I kept my thin dime
Away from those treacherous waters
Where the view is straight down.

Here Today

In a quick tan rush
The sex of a great palm
Falls off with a clatter.

My cat is nine tenths asleep
And wakes for a moment
Then returns nine tenths asleep.

I have fallen asleep too
Reading a book on the stars
Complete with photographs.

Islands of neon still
Swim on black space in my mind.

And I could say at this point
Some moral like all
Sex falls away at some point.

That would be smaller
Than any thought I have had
In the last vast half hour

But would sell the poem
To most readers of poems,
Satisfying their expectations

That a poem should be somehow
Humane and applicable to their own
Longings and carings about the mundane.

Ah me. Ho Hum. Well a day.
Phrases of letting the damned world
Slide. I heave my sigh, too,

And go back to the book
Complete with exposures of
Where all of us really spend our time.

South Beach When

When Fish Mary talks you listen,
If you're smart, and say little.
A nod here and an expression there
That tells her she knows when,
Will do. And then the tales come:
The Firpo fight, the wooden pier,
How she was painted gold one night.

For a beer. Or two. You
Leave the change if you're smart.

Myself, I've spent forever peering
Into imaginary corners. I know when.

Federated Stores

Oh, *that* Lazarus. You mean Ralph
Lazarus, Chairman of Merchants, Boss
Of Profits. I thought you meant

Emma Lazarus, who wrote under
The pedestal of Liberty,
Give me your tired, give me your
Poor. But you meant Ralph.

I know what you're thinking.
You're thinking about *the* Lazarus
Stirring in the shroud, breathing
Again after the long stillness.

What percentage, Ralph would say,
Is there in that?

Salutations

There we go again,
Calling it a colony
Of ants, when
Most all are the same person.

Clones, not colony
Would be the proper
Form of address.

The truth is as if
A thousand John Aldens
Bespoke one Priscilla.

Shades of Plymouth Rock, why
Even a queen would blush
At such inaccurate naming.

And this raises questions
About anyone's founding,
How many individuals ever
Make a city.

Metaphysical

The bleached skull of a sea turtle,
His beaked jaw intact,
Braces the end of my bookshelf.
A dried framed butterfly graces
The other, and in between
Tomes from Math to Medical.
M. There must be a Moral.

From Death to Death commentary
Suspends, a long catenary.
That is unnaturally forced.
Say all life serves to bind
Our thoughts together. That
Would be inexact and grandiose.

Images rise: out of the green
Surf the mortal shell hurls
Its drab weight on the sand.
Or a flicker of color in the net.
Net. In there somewhere.
Between a minnow of the air
And a slow sea flier. The

Net. What is the net weight
Of this all? Some words we
Breathe. Some slim ideas
That swim unusual currents.
Inaccurate dreams about
The airs of other worlds.

Forty

Stuffed-up nose, scratchy throat, I
Ache, says the man in the pajamas.

How about me? So many words have
Scuffed my throat over the years,
Tears and sniffles upon the page,
Poem after poem popping like Kleenex.

What a way to earn a life. And now
His wife says, take this ampule, this
Capsule, this pill. Well, Hell, where's

My panacea, doll, friend, wife, girl,
Anyone? I could stand a suppression
Of symptoms: less welling up of the
Heart, less fever pitch, fewer visions.

Bed Time Story

I float on water, unable to sleep.
Light sounds of the house abound:
Timbers sigh as the house cools.
Somewhere I hear the claws of the cat.

Even the rigid house must take its ease
In small motions and sounds of the night.

Quickly I am very awake: the knives
Have turned their edges up. Behind
The clockfaced cupboard door,
The gun eases its safety off. A
House is dangerous. I fall asleep.

The Dania Pier

Someone has caught a hideous fish,
Spiny and speckled,
Dull brown and battleship grey,
Nothing anyone would stuff on a wall.

Never having seen anything like it,
And not caring either,
The lucky fisher has already rebaited.
Neighbors turn back to their own trickeries.

And the fish
Dries slowly on the wooden deck
Not even gasping.

It seems a day for negatives.
The sky brown and spiny.

While the Moon Is Listening

Three hundred pounds one hundred fifty years
Giganticus the turtle claws into the beach
And dies a straining outstretched drowning
Death clumsy as a strange sculpture.

Once
In Africa
A wooden idol
Carved by the most imaginative of the carvers
(Beyond his own guessing, past his gods)
A wooden turtle out of stone.

All carvers stepped a step back into themselves
Into their own wooden art
Into each chop they ever skillful cut.

To cut the stone itself?
To cut the rock of the world?
To shape the world?
Once
In Africa

And here
Three hundred pounds one hundred fifty years
Lifts all his life and dies upon the tide the
Tide while

The moon is listening like a stone

The Ghost of Polonius

Yes directly in the stomach
Slightly above the navel if I remember right
And yes

I would stink up the stone
Never to be quite scrubbed from the memory
Of the noses of the courtiers.

Of course it was the wrong place to have been standing
Nosey, and then the blade came nosing.
I never cried out, did they tell you that?

Never.
A good politician, I knew death
In a hundred appointments and clamberings.
Past a thousand I scurried to the top,
Whispering about assassination,
Until Claude
Did it.

How we drank that night knowing we backed
The right man.

Don't sneer at my proverbs.
I was close to it all as a man can come and,
I remind you,

Nearer to Hamlet than you.

Moonflight II

Having picked men
Of no imagination
And censoring even them

We got what we asked for:

Photos of ourselves in color,
At a long distance.

Couldn't make out any faces,
Got bored,
Went back to the bridge game

That also crossed Nothing.

Extra Vehicular Activity

Got off the wheelchair,
Caught hold of the bannister,
Pulled himself up the stairs
By his biceps,

Dragging the usual lap robe,

All the way to the bathroom

Rather than foul himself.

Later the story
Amused the nurses.
Especially the part about how
He had to face the wrong way.

It became known
As the Daylight Ride.

But only
In ambulatory.

The Day after the New Year

A few green needles have fallen.
Another tree is over.

The woman who lives with me
Takes down her decorations.

Once again death has lifted itself
Up almost into the room.

I wonder what the temperature is
And go to look.

So much as that?

Blackbeard

At the tip of the plank
He turned to look at the crew
And knew

All about exile, how

It can get you strolling the streets of Nassau.
It can take you up short in the Bermudas.
It swells in the eyes of your fellows.

Obedience has two honed edges.

When he tried to get back aboard
They slashed at him like barracuda.

At the tip of the plank
His wrists tugged at the hemp.
He cried
And wet the front of his pants.

Exile

Is the empty dominion.

Bulldozer

On Iwo and Tarawa the busy Seabees
Wore masks making mass graves.

Where dark smokes masked
Only the small white puffs of bone
Snapping
Like the sound of faroff rifles.

Today the pollen silently puffs
On the calcium breeze
Over the atolls built, I am told,
Of the builtup skeletons of the sea.

Exo Endo Exo, says the tide
To the tides of the ear.

Ta ta ta ta ta ta tatata tatata
The Eyes and Ears of the World

The End

Paramount News

Last Man on the Moon

It was sweat on the way out,
Fog on the facemask,
Damp under arms.
Bells rang in my dreams
Within a dream.
The soft glow of eyebrow lighting
Reddened greened and blued my eyes.

It was sweat, it was worry whether
Timimg was split   as a second.

It was Be calm, it was Be alert,
It was like flying any new machine:
Steady, Steady. It was rhythm
And shudder. It was burn, burn.
It was pressure.

Slow moments en route we played:
Would we touch down? Or up?
Was our time real?
Where had the certainties all gone?

The jokes were queries
No machine could answer.

Then we arrived.

And touching (it was down) the moon,
We found it one more foreign airport,
Flying the lander, one more first solo.

You climb out feeling proud and shaky,
Look about for someone to take notice
That wonders happen in broad daylight.
The formula: mild disappointment over joy.

There is walking around to get your legs.
The moon suits have a colder air.
The damp inside feels frozen.
The earth is overhead and still.

Coming back was even smoother,
Pressures, burns and pounds remaining,

Splashing down and heavy arms
Pressing the final clumsy buttons.

And we are here, you see,
Chatting over coffee
As if the whole flight never had occurred.
As if all traveling so minutely planned,
No room for wander in the slightest sense,
Leaves nothing for the memory.

We sit. We talk to you. We see
Ourselves raising our programmed hands.

We analyze our time left on
This blue and white and shining globe.

It was a picnic on a star.
It was no picnic on a star.

We are all travelers through space,
No matter what our standpoint.

I truly have no more to say to you.
Brother, we speed the heavens.

Einstein at the Cafe Bulwark

Kepler was dead. Galileo was dead.
Newton. Nothing to do
But go back and forth to the Patent Office,
Thinking upon novelty.

Travelers Inn

The waitress is being teased
About a boy she has been to bed with.
Her customers watch her face
For the small wrinkles near the eyes
To tell them what to say next.

They see how the mind moves.
How there can be no tone no sound
But turning say
As a heavy flag turns
Or shifting
As in old fires.

They tell her a preposterous tale.
Well, she says, you know that Frank
And then stares for a moment
Into the wash water.

The poem and the face.
They are to see how the mind moves.

Caesar Poet

The first civilization took
Over ten thousand years,
The next fewer.

And now with each generation
Civilizations are upon us.
And in the future?

All Egypt in a year.

Rome built in a day.

Magic

I had not full reckoned on the icy current
Said Houdini.

It took two days
To thaw a hole with my breath.

I had a stronger
Wish / heart / desire to be sure

Nothing, no man, could hold me,
Not even my own body.

Nights
I picked at the moon.

The doctor was frightened.
The Great Glass Bottle Escape!
But finally he

Hinged my ribcage,
Sawed my collarbones,
Swiveled my hips,

It all depends on
How far one will go.

And I said,
Nights I picked at the moon

Touring in the Mountains

Turning away, the veterans yawn
Like caves they've wasted dollars on:
The cliff is nice. The stairs are steep.
It's just another Lover's Leap.

Unseen, the sun is in decline.
The mountains flash their timberline.
Each hometown poet, I suppose,
Comes down from honeymoon to prose.

In Florida

A boy in a field nearby whistles his dog
And the dog comes fetching a stick
Too wide for his mouth, and the boy
Lifts him off his feet and swings
That dog around in circles containing
No *let go.*

I lived in the woods of Alaska long
Enough to know the cold that comes
To the trees at night, that can
Freeze a stream solid like a giant
Icicle laid on the ground. Knew
The cold enough to feel it
Seep through wool and fur and
Chill the body's hair. There was
One word the skin spoke then and
It is still here under the flood
Of sun. That dog knows well the
Word through his canine teeth
To his rigid tail.
Those two syllables are one word
Still. *Hang on.*

Diagnoses

Criminal, this. The good doctor
Explains that apparently there is
Nothing wrong, that even under
Strange rays it doesn't show.

The psychiatrist leans back
Furthest in his chair and says,
Tell me of your childhood. Christ,
I thought I'd told everyone about
Those early hours, or tried.

Inside, where it counts, the bones
Keep parting and snapping with
Every move: the spine itself
And its guy wires give. Hell
Seems working its way out

The thing is, I don't know what
I'm coming to, and I can't help
Myself, while the brain hovers
Over me like a mother, worrying.

I go on, We all go on. I can't
Help but wonder, how many others
Twist in their own juices like
This, are crabbed in their gait.

When I started out on this journey,
Who could have figured? What if
Nothing is wrong, the horrible
Only normal? Mercy, mercy.

Garbage Can Blues

This head once knew a satin bed
And afternoons of bliss

So look to your lovers ladies
Rub and pet and kiss

Cause Purr is how it ought to be
Meow is how it is

Ask any cat who aint too fat
He'll tell you in a whiz

Purr is how it ought to be
Meow is how it is

The Poet as a Contemporary Reflection

A brass pot full of dry flowers
Hangs in the mirror while I dine.
The pot is flecked with tarnish,
The spotted patina of age.

After coffee, I turn to leave.
The pot hangs in my eyes, brand new and shining.

Outside, on the drive home,
A mirror hangs in my head,
An old mirror, its silver tarnished,

Flecked with brass reflections.

The Dream Ants

Talk about hopes. I am barely
Attempting to shave, and across the clean
Formica is a run of ants up early
Moving the brown shell of an insect.
Must be breakfast. Beetle over easy.

The razor nicks my chin. Close.
The way I feel, it scraped suicide,
Surfacing from the perfect arms, perfect lady,
Perfect small island all tan blue and green.
I put the blade down to brush up
The teeth, the hair. Look:
One ant has stopped to sip blood.

Wisps of dream still cloud my eyes,
Steam the mirror. But that ant
Prefigures a thoroughly evolved Great
Bathroom Ant, who eats soap, hair,
Drinks razor blood, breathes steam.
His rain falls from metal inside glass.
His feet pace pure tile and chrome.

I towel my face and the vision clears.
I cannot face the kitchen, mainly
The stainless disposal which eats eggshells.

A line of white ants has carried my dreams away.
There is something to carry everything away.

Abstraction Blooded

You know the phantom limb, how
The brain remembers reach,
Touch, how
The empty pinned sleeve
Snaps on the light,
Buttons the vest tight.

I know the phantom body,
Scratch my own back
As the good book says,
Then high over head
Catgut slams the fuzzy ball.
Ace!
      Or no point at all.

Programs of the person,
Unthinking knots of tie, oh
How patiently hand taught the mind.

Spirit is telling, telling me I need
No fingertips to feel,
No legs to run
Beyond the moon, beyond the sun.

Showing My Age (21 Genes)

1

The bells on my feet ring fool as I walk
I drool with intelligence at the world
Here I come mother
Here I come martyr
Here I come politico

Spine twisted with indignation

Oh knot of it all
Riddle
Ribbon wind
Moebius spin returning returning

The bells on my feet ring fool
My gait in the world is halt

2

The tree ascends to the left

In the long-spun grope for sun

The man ascends to the right
Spun by his arm out stretched

The natural politics:

One man, one tree.

3

As I turn my morning faces to the world

Smiling like warm toast

As I wrap my ears about sound in the front
Eyes around
What is it the eyes are around?

Coax me up into here sweet light

Up from the earth for what reason
Up from the damn you know where

4
Don't listen to this
Man out of his skull

A man whom every neutered cat
Does his sidewise dances at

My house is inside the head
Bonecave

I grew up in a duplex
Imagine the next generation

Left right left right left right
Left.

Old splitbrain,
Come to attention.

5
The left handed man has been used to a world
Where the doors conspire against him

Said the lady fluffing a pillow

My stays and my stops and my snaps and my straps
Were stiched by a
Left handed seamstress
From left handed cloth with a left handed cut

Said the lady fluffing her tresses

The left handed man and the right handed man
Are totally different lovers

Said the lady to her kitty

And she fluffed his bow of satin ribbon
And his purr pronounced him pretty

6
Right hander come off the left foot honey

Left hander fumble at the door

I am the pretty tricky

Dance you toward the door

Right hander
Got a hitch and fumble

Left hander step the wrong way

I got a juggle handy
Smooth as the taste of candy

Always new and never before

7

Watch a left handed lover
Grab you from the blind side

Left handed lovah baby
He aint got no pride

Now a right handed lover
Will leave you torn

So I'm a both handed darlin
With a two cheek grab

All bone and muscle
And the gift of gab

8

The opposable thumb
Precedes the opposable lobes

Or vice versus

Obviously the answer to the oldest riddle is

The egg came first
The egg of the pre chicken

Historic
Day

Glad tidings for roosters

In a small way
We are a new species each

9

Ah, says the brilliant worm,
I feel about to become new.

Rebirth is like that, says the saint.

What was that terrible dream?
Says the butterfly.

10

We ooh we ooh goes
The tremulo of the night
My heart is pulled
Over

Red speeder
Where did you think
You were going?

Don't feed me stale
Excuses like love

Don't tell old yarns
Of fresh desire

I could have warned you
You were heading for
A fire

11

My photos (till now) show the throw
Of weight to the left heel,

The right eye sights over the nose.

Balance balanced.

Characteristic, says the deoxyribo
Nucleic acid,
How you stand it.

I better change the way I
Strut my stuff.

12

Big program

How do you want me?

Big program,
How shall I go?

With liberal style
And conservative smile

And toilet training down below?

Big program,
How do you want me?

Big program,
Where shall I grow?

In outer space, at inner pace,

In the spin of the big eeeeee Go?

13

O_2 eddies into the blood,

Snatches a lift on the hemoglobin,

Tumbles

Splash in the blood of the stream,

Slides through the wall of the cell,

And oh

Two

Hon

Is what you mean to me.

14

Dear Mr Moebius,

I try to contain myself but
Some days my right handed chromosome
Take my breath away

Why my left incisor over
Laps the
Right why
I pivot on that heel too

Right hand fumbles with its food
Left hand hangs on for dear
Life

I think
How *come* I think?
How *come* dextrous?
How come *come*?

I try to contain my

Right brain running the left side
Left brain crossing right
Oh corpus callosum
Meeting of minds

Out of flat matter
How you shape space how

I try to contain my
There I go again

15

Suddenly the skull and crossbones
Leaps out.

The crossed arms,
The empty eyes,
Teeth naked to the air,

Mother under the skin,
Mirror,

Welcome me in.

I'll have to thin
Have to go gossamer.

I'll have to get *I'll* again,
Find me over.

It's the blues Mister Einstein,
(We never met)

The deep black
Middle of the night time
The when you were a kid
Waking up to nowhere
Crying out blues.

I don't know when to stop
I don't know when to stop
If I live it any longer
I think I'm gonna drop.

16

You all know Ohm
His right hand is a law and a half

Ohm Om see under Eeeee
Lectricity see under

Buddhism

This is the way the current goes
The current goes
The current goes

Good sense of time has Mister Einstein
He may catch on

You have to be a little plant
Before you are a flower

You have to be a rose afire
Under the summer hour

You have to have a pair of eyes
Lifting toward the sun but

The bright lights of our birthdays
Flicker and are done

I try to contain

Not even pause pauses

17

Mr Moebius, my math is humming.
I stare out of your field.

The steep cliffs of proposition unwind
Unwind:

The double helix of the hour's glass crosses
The infinity in a grain of sand.

The crystals are singing the very
Truth is sunning.

Antagonistic muscles,
Tense me tight.

18

All the moon's a stage

The nucleotides
Mosh and pother

The hydrogen bond is twinning
Plus looking in the mirror
Plus yearning minus

The moon's our mother
The sun's our father

The earth's our author
Time's our tether and

All the sea's a page

I know

The continents wander
The great S of the hemispheres

Lag under the spin

Resistance
Slow as Andrew Marvell watching a leaf

You are always
Reminding reminding

I know
Of the earth's red center

Enough to cook
Oceans

Fry devils

See their tails thrash

19

Eye tooth
Where have you led me?
Bite
What do you want?
Taste?

And you down there
Hustler
Smooth talker

Spit it out.

Grow up,
Says the DNA.
Stand straight.

20

All though
We was taut
(That's singer's grammar)
"Man is bilaterally summetrical"

Bi *Helically* Symmetrical, Mama,

Is the Truth,

Is the Sonlight,

Is what I say.

21

Two selves
Two lobes

Di Lemma, Mama

Two sides (like questions)
Two faces (like lovers)

Mitosis of the mind

I favor the organic, but
Will settle for the in.

Elapsed rhyme, I'm.

Fact is, I'm

                                      grounded
                                      attracted
                                      repulsed
                                      pulsed

Look deep in my pupils!
Do you see ocean?
Do you see fire?

Shall I spell me out?

I can feel the blueback of my retina.

Old soft touch,
Blinding day,

Now bring me the invisible world.

Living Proof
(1985)

Ocean

The gray falls down to green. The line
Of sky is dimming. Lights
Bob up curve down curve up. The
Self dips. We
Are stars at sea
Swimming.

Opening Poem

The first poem in the book should be
The best poem in the book and we
Better be brought up to snuff.
No fooling. Give us
The crack shot, top measure,
No dandelion on the lawn.

Each line should snap like a spinnaker
Or a noose. Nothing halfway.
Mother should peer out at us.
We ought not be able to finish it
Without glancing around
Or shifting our seat.

The whole wash should hang out heavy,
The sun should glare hot on it,
We should smell the damp in our breath,
Color should bloom like a flowerbed,
And we should know with pure faith
Life will whip in the wind by afternoon.

Vincent, Vincent

The green blue walls open wide
Like a book. The red brown floor
Tiles fall like a sprung trap door.
The sunflower chair is hurled at you.
Its color held him like a bee.

All day his brain turned slowly with the sun.
He sat silent as Midas. Even
The hot French wind on his face was yellow.
No wonder he got lost in a starry night. But
That chair is carved from flower stuff.

Gold enough, gold enough.

Paul Gauguin

I know why you had to leave. He
Loved you, but saw through everything.
He was so alone, except for God shining down,
The need for man was utter. Side by side,
Scene by scene, you were becoming a vanishing

Point. And then the second chair: all that
Evident love in the curve and the color. So much so
You lost you, sailing away for your dear life, but
Dear Paul, your absence fills that empty chair,
While deep in your green jungle,

His eye is the leopard's eye.

Ages

It was Louis Pasteur, I believe,
Who wasted almost one year
With his eye to a powerful lens
Trained on a little dish.

With a needle he moved a powder:
All the righthanded crystals left,
All the lefthanded crystals right,
Two tiny teaspoons of crystals.

Imagine him there, scarcely breathing,
Not a feather of wind in the room,
Teasing his crystals with needles
Into two tiny peaks on the dish.

It took him almost a year,
Student Pasteur with his needles.
And then, of course, the announcement
For which, of course, no one waited:

All living crystals are
Righthanded crystals. And
Righthanded crystals only.
The rest of the universe
Mixes its crystals. Life

Is righthanded, righthanded.

That experiment now is buried
Under the dust of the thousands
Of long dull laboratory hours,
Most of them yielding no answers,
Or, what is worse, no questions.

It is all a matter of finding.
Or not finding. No one remembers
The aching neck of young Louis
Holding his breath in a room,
Holding his fingers so steady,

In an Age when, we say, life was slower.

Black Hole
for Stephen Hawking

You remind me of a curious vine.
No matter what, it grew as it grew
And played itself out lightward,
Climbing up and upon some lack.

By twining about an absence,
It raised a green question
As a flute will a cobra.

So your song curls around silence:
Either nothing is right there or
Something is not right there.

If I could code precise words
To what I am surely not saying,
We would fathom the utter darkness
Between fact and fact, but

My figure is easy as your figure:
Aside from the sense of humor,
There is absolutely nothing to it.

Robert Frost

He held himself apart until the man
Was the last rustic. Rockers creak
When you read him, boulders balance.

The final lines of his poems
Fall like an avalanche, seen
With the sound turned down.

We turn down sound.
We turn down poets and their lives.

I put the complete poems back on the shelf to yellow
Like a sheaf of pressed

Flowers from another summer,
Index my spectacles,

And peer again at the computer
Screen. The color words are flying like
A flock of butterflies on a mown field.

Men work together, I tell him from the heart,
Whether they work together,
Or apart.

Chicopee River

There is no reason
Why this memory
Should open like a yellow umbrella,
Dry in the downpour,

But I am there, a boy
Sliding the hundreds of feet
Down the hot sand banks of the Chicopee
Where they shine in the summer's sun
Like the top half of a huge
Hourglass.

Young, I am young,
And I rush with the young down
Long rides upon the cardboard sleds.
I can even see close
My worn-through canvas shoes.

Fifty does that. More
And more, old times are clear as
Magnified print, while

The moments of today
Drop like the coins
Of a boy with a hole
In his pocket.
It is pouring and pouring here,
Hard as sand from a shoe.

I shall hold tight to this desk,
As we fly fast as a dream
From moment to moment to moment
Back up the quicksilver river
Even as far as Indian Bend.

My mother is there.
And my father.

Living and living and living.

Prayer

Like it or not,
We like our wild things in a pot.

We turn the green face from the sun
For symmetry, we say, for
Balance. One

Skeptic might suspect
Another simple need of Man
For order in the growth of God.

We trim the sod, we clip
Clip the bushes, underlining that the tree
In truth knows East and West
As well as we.

And it tastes darkness at the root.
And at the leaf the sunny absolute.

Oh God who turns my mind first
This then that
Way, please

Give me my bright way. For I
(And certainly it is my doom)
Feel a short quarter-inch from
(May I call it)

Bloom?

Artificial Intelligence

Euclid rolled over in his bones
When Newell & Simon instructed
Their machine to look for new proof
For bisecting the ordinary triangle.

No one at all expected
Except perhaps Newell & Simon
The machine to say something unheard of.

But it did. And there
Was the glorious proof, never dreamed
By any mathematician, but
I ask you, Newell & Simon,

How can any imagine that somewhere
Inside a triangle turned
Over, one side as a hinge?
Or was there even a triangle?
Or even a line or a point?
Or even a sharpened formula?
Or even the thought of a shape?

Was there any joy in the crystals?
Any Aha or Eureka?
How sad, Misters Newell & Simon,
That no one awoke in a sweat,
Making inherent coherent,
So the living are left to explain
How an inanimate universe
Can contrive to make itself plain.

Words for Jesus of Nazareth

I

My heart hangs
Hangs on a curve between two beating pains
Slung in a red hammock
Tossing in dreams of a future

I know I am a man
To breathe is to crush the heart

Spittle runs from the eyebrow
Down the cheek to the beard
Cold trace

I know I am a man the nails
Divining rods

The penis a crushed ache
Up from
I know I am a man
The fear behind their faces
In their whips
Hangs

Too long
Pray

II

Hums rise
Light rises

Dark the wet womb

And the great stone of birth to roll back

III

Heaven the unblemished manhood

IV

The smooth cool wood I remember
Oil sliding my palm on the shine
The shavings of sweet freshness

And the call away I remember

The long life of tasks
The clear image of fate in the well

Water for the desert
Kisses for the lepers

      V

I know I am a man

Hung

Up

Side

Down

Florida

We are South looking North.
Or vice versa.
We are international
And exceptionally local.

From here you could go to the moon.
And we can prove it.

Even the natives are transients.
Arriving and departing,
We are of two minds.

Coast to coast here means
One hour through our cotton mountains.
The sun rises and sets under salt waters.

Knowing in the bones that space is time,
We are wise as any peninsula.
We mine the dried beds of forgotten seas.
Fresh mango and orange bloom from the silt.

Outside Gainesville once, I reached down
Into time and touched the saber tooth of a tiger.
No atlas prepared me for the moist
Sweet smell of his old life.

Suddenly a flock of flamingos
Posed a thousand questions,
Blushing like innocence.
But the moon, perfectly above Miami
Like some great town clock, whispers,
"Now . . . yesterdays . . . tomorrows . . . "

And standing tropically and hugely still
At this port of meditation,
Reduced to neither coming nor going,
We are together on the way to somewhere.

In good time.

Tutankhamen Traveling

With no perspective, I sit like the true Egyptian.
Flat, I am become the scene and the wall.
As far as your curved eye can see,
Thousands of me line the hall.

And I ask you what you expected to find:
Was it the round earth or the round mind?

My world is infinitely open forever.
My journey never ends. Nothing ever returns
Upon itself. The white clouds sail the blue,
The blue, forming the blue, vanishing,

Suddenly it is raining everywhere at once.
There is never anything but now going on.

Tell me, shall my mask speak golden truths?
Tell me, where will you leave your face?

I shall always sit in a spectacular desert,
My civilization about me like a cloak.

Gulliver

The nostril was familiar
Long grey hair curling out and away
Then the wart on the cheek next to the wrinkle
He knew it then

His face it was he crawled
Could feel the tickle looked down
There he was near the wart and wrinkle

How could this be
Finding oneself sticky with satire
Lessened and lessoned

Own features blown
Heady with headings

The answer came searching and found him
Empuzzled

Time upon time the most super imposure
Face after face mirror on mirror

Math after math after math after math

Poem for Wyatt Wyatt

Satan,
Having mulled things over
In a frigid clime,
Had decided that next time
(And make no mistake about it)
He was gonna get God good.

Having bided,
Opportunity knocked its once
And God went down
Past absolute zero
To where he belonged,
As Satan put it.

We all make mistakes,
Said God, departing heaven,
But before the Devil
Had counted to, say, seven,

God's GOD appeared
In a puff of red plasma gas,
Saying to Satan,
Not bad, but . . .

Your idea of heaven is not the last
Idea of heaven.

Janice

If she were a goddess and we told her story
We would say Death had fallen in love
And reaching around to hold her close
One of his powerful fingers had slipped in.

The cancer they took out from her back
Looked like a finger the doctor agreed
Though he had to send away for a name
To discover whether the touch was malign.

She must wait a week and we must wait a week
To find in a message from a white laboratory
If that fellow's intentions are sincere
And how the family will act if he asks her hand.

Morning

The local priest floats by in his blue car.
He is in no hurry and the radio is on loud.
He, for one, has never done one thing wrong.
He is in heaven already. Life is a long ritual.

Meanwhile, on the porch screened against flies,
This poet sits biting his quick, sipping caffeine,
Smoking one cigar after another. Smoky as Hell.
Life to him scarcely makes anything out clearly.

The moral is, and everything either has or hasn't
A moral, the moral is, count your blessings
Without anyone watching. And on your knees.
Hell is waiting for everyone who sits too easy.

Florida Turnpike

Green scrub plain against a cyan sky,
White clouds, white highway, and
You began to sing, Eubie Blake,
Of yourself and your shadow
And that avenue in New York.

Now you are a shade, Eubie,
Even your notes fall on my ears
Like little bird shadows

In the elevator, out of hearing of
Joe Franklin and the camera,
You extended those long black fingers,
Made chords in the air,
And gave me an eighty-year-old wink,
Saying, "Just me
And my shadow."

You are gone, Eubie Blake.
I am your shadow.

Memo of Compliance
for Steve Altman

Yes, yes, yes, another report
Of how I am fulfilling something
Or other: please believe, I mean
No disrespect, but these people
I have been sent among. Their
Alphabet is odd. Their God,
Even, I cannot understand.

Christ, in fact, any Messiah,
Is so far from their understanding
(Or their wish) . . .

I would you knew them as I
Try to know them, Barbarians
Is not even apt. They seem
To worship. They seem to
Pray. But I cannot keep
Even close to accurate accounts
Of what I have done, accomplished,
Or what I intend to do
Tomorrow, if I have the chance.

I know you need some justification
Of why I have been sent here,
Some rationale of your position
Keeping me on . . . I'm at a loss
To answer more than that I try,
Or hope to try, or plan perhaps,
To start to try, or learn to
Begin to try . . . harder? (Is that
What you want, or think you want,
From me, or what I was, at least?)
Or shrewder, or more successfully?
I do keep up. Some days I don't know
What I keep. Barbarians, I said.
It's not just that. They seem
To have a culture all their own.

Values, maybe. Or maybe what
We imagine are values.

I need . . . vacation? I am already
Vacant in some ways. Write me,
Please. But no more reports,
Understand, or be prepared for
Suspicions of what I do, or
Might do. Believe the rumors.
I am doing everything imaginable
To sustain myself. And you.
Whoever I am. Or you are.
Best. Sincerely. Yours.
Respectfully, whatever that means.

Key Largo

It is nothing like the movie.
No one here bets the horses,
Certainly not Fancy free.

Even the slow long-bladed fans
Are gone. Only champagne and pompano
Still go together.

In the rest of the country, well.
Rocco still runs things.
We still count the votes
Until they come out right.

As Bogey says, he was just
Passing through.

Time Study
for Romeo Skellings

Romeo would stopwatch Love,
The Night Super was found of saying.
But my father went clicking along,
Charting the motions of manufacture,
And one day a man from the government
Raised a blue flag with a golden E.
There was a short ceremony
And then they went back to war.

I have mused about this at some
Length, studying how to get
Idea in fit words, whether or when
I could sneak a smoke in the Men's room.

Most of my friends go leisurely about
Inattentive to the Efficiency of Nature,
So you see it does pose a problem.
Should one do this or that first?
Can one eliminate waste
Movements of the mind in the maze?
When is good enough toward perfection?

He is with me always, frowning Not Bad, Not
Bad. Yeats is there, too, the two
Conniving geezers worrying if
My last word has a well quit snap.

Her Class Reunion
for Lolita Skellings

So little history is ever set
In the bold black and white of books.

Sigh for the moments never set down,
Sigh for the moments almost forgotten.

It is like coming suddenly from the hot sun
Into the cool of the bookstore, browsing,
Turning the pages of a strange history,
Coming upon your own face in an old photo.

I didn't remember I was there! Look, there's . . .
What was his name? And her, now. Remember?

It is like coming from the hot sun of today
Into the cool book of history. Can it be
That long ago? Listen! Fifty years
Is the hinge of the Century. Soon its
Great door will close, so,

Open the pages, quick, open them wide,

(For the children only learn of generals
And presidents, of battlefield and marketplace,
Years reduced to numbers . . .)

Open the real history. See? We are there,
Walking quietly home from school,
Waving to friends,
Waiting for trolleys,
Admiring the new car, and the talk, remember?
Remember those long fast hours
In the green shade of the trees?

(And the children, bored, can shut our book,
And we can shut our book, take the deep breath
Of Tomorrow . . .)

But we were together.
And we are again together.
And we will always be together.

The Bells

for Harold and Constance Crosby

Gathered here, we make a church.

And something in the memory
Rhymes. Remember

Leaping upon the air, the long
Slow pull upon the rope, the give
And fall. Our bodies

Brought down tones upon the town.

Now these two bells.
These two bells here
In tune in time.

Oh, leap upon the air, for
To tune two bells against the din
And clamor of our everydays,

Each ringer, chimer, rhymer, tells
The toll. But toils. And tolls.

We sound against the dark, against
Our fears, we sound

Not melody, but sympathy.

Oh, tones together, chime.
Above the warring of the sexes, chime.
Above the squabble of the nations, chime.

Oh love that rings above all time,
That makes time needless but to ring upon,
Tell One plus One

Be One.

Against that dark, against
Those fears, against all going, go
To bed for all of us tonight, tonight
And everynight. Oh,
Chime.

Courses

The rattan fan blades follow
Each other round and round and
Round and occasionally
I catch their drift.

They are something like my friends,
Stiff in their courses,
Circling one another,
Their innards are silent.

Their intent is imperceptible:
Lazily hypnotic, crazily repetitive,
One could grow quite mad guessing
What grand hyperbolas
Those blades might follow

If all power and all hell
Broke loose.

Eye Teeth

At the bell I bring my bag of sweets
And open the door to a flock of ghosts.
One particular black vampire sneers,
Showing formidable green wax fangs.
I smile. Good show. They each select
A Milky Way. I make them take a tangerine.

The ghosts vanish into the night. I sit,
Awaiting the next set of ghouls, sucking
My hard candy. Last Hallowed Eve
The fiends were at the door for hours,
More frightening than they knew,
Caricatures of our bestial past,
Funny displays of instinct.

I looked up at a Palm Beach dinner once,
Thinking of nothing except cutlery and
All were showing their teeth with smiles
And biting down on flesh and chewing.
The expensive veneer of civilization
Fell away, then, and I swigged the white wine.

Get away from the door, goblins, scat
Skeletons, back back back black witches.
You can't turn unreal what I know is real.
I go to the plain unenchanted mirror.
The ghosts of all my ancestors look back.

Statuesque

I have been an inhabiter of statues,
That strange disease of looking
Through their patient eyes.

From Rushmore I gaze, and out
Sphinxish, on the blank sand.

Deep, under the sea called
Mediterranean, I am the silent
Christ of the Abysses, blessing
The deaths of divers.

High in the Andes, I look out
Over the bay of Rio.

Horses leap under me. Great
Snakes battle my muscles.
I am beautiful as Adonis.

Translated into marble,
I will live forever.

Vocals

Cats cry like babies to get a pet.
Dog mimics dog to bark think twice.
Bears rumble growls to fur the cave.
Wolves howl solace across the ice.

Words that fit so well are few.
When you cried today, I cried too.

Free Climbing

By fifty-three one ought to be depressed.
I got it over with by forty. Doc said,
Sounds as if you yearn for Mount Olympus.

Damn tooting. I soloed round the lesser stones:
Deborah, Hess, Hayes, even McKinley,
Stared in a green glacier a million years.

Settling for pebbles after is demeaning.
Might as well go to the nearest moon.
I shuddered off both doctor and depression,

So in my sixties I'd be elevated
As well as get, somehow someway by Jove,
That god damned rocky mountain recreated.

Clear Moon

Footprints on the moon are prints of feet
In the mind only. Much may be seen
By this method, my brothers, antique
Though it seem. Poets get deft
And half daft with such looking.

Youth may loom close this way,
Stay prepared for tears:
Summer lovers, sunshine friends,
The eye of the traitor before and after.

And take this warning from one well practiced:
Hindsight is foresight. Don't wander or

Look ahead like a greedy lizard,
Look back like a god on an ape.

Notes on Relative Inertia

And now too late as usual
The physics professor tells me
Everything depends on everything else.

For without the distant stars
Objects in motion would not (necessarily)
Remain in motion.

I would have to keep throwing the ball.
Nothing would fall. Push
Would come to shove.

There would be no rest for the wicked
Or anyone. No body could get on
In the world. Or any where.

Most likely in the next lesson
Where will go. If there is go.
So you and me love better make hay

While the sun shines.

News Brief

Nothing happened today. Yesterday
Sat like a pool ball rack. If
You were shocked by the headline,
Stunned by photograph, electrified
By bloody details from the bandaged survivor,
Blame the loose set, damp chalk,
Bad cue, even the uneven table.

It wasn't your scratch. It wasn't
From your genes, nature, or nurture.
You were not odd. Blame it on God.

Driver Ed

Everyone pulls the shining colorfully painted
Automobile he paid an arm and a leg for
Over to the side of the road and then off the road
And leans the hot forehead against the cool steering wheel
Once in his young life.

That's the last chapter, chum:
No sense turning back, no point pushing on.
And you are learning a lesson about the top speed of life
That none of the experts rushing by can help with.

Nuclear

The atom is not like a ring
Of marbles. No no, nor
Some great knuckler must
Be imagined, huge knees
Hunkered down. God's ass
In the air, eyes intent
On a smoky blue agate
Should not be thought of.

Nor the planets like
Oranges spinning in orbits
From jugglers, think upon.

For the mind will hunker down,
Then. Or spin.

Vision instead those old carved ivory
Chinese globes within globes
Within globes. Use your long
Fingernail to inspect the
Interiors. Latticed within
Lattice, so thin they are held
Together by their own holding.

The electron is nowhere. Rather
It is not anywhere, rather it is
Its shell, rather it is almost
A shell. Shell within shell
Whispers like a shoreline.
From shell to shell the
Shushing goes. Passage
Is all there is of is.

Gladiatorial

We, who are about to die, Caesar,
Salute you, because such is the nature
Of bureaucracy, military or any other ary.
We know you enjoy the differential
Twixt physical deference and mental
Detestation. By Jupiter, you sure do get
Your toga up over similar tensions. We
Desire you lionized, but bow behind
Swords and nets. Plenipotentiaries, know this:
Half a chance, different birth, dice
In our favor, muscle would muscle flab, we'd
The gift of gab, ours the flag, the name,
The game. Meanwhile, we die for you over
The leftover, hank of zebra, leopard hair,
Meek to inherit the last hack of the earth.

Senior Citizen

My dad decided he would burn.
His buddies always said he would.
His tailor did him as he should
And hot flame fit him to a turn.

Far, oh far, as I can tell
He's running rum or chasing fur
In heaven or perhaps in hell.
My father read dice as they fell.

Things were for him the way they are
And are tonight the way they were.
Fool? Fool. Star? Star.
He always loved a bright red car.

What he lived was all he learned.
My dad decided to be burned.

Carnival

Your youth is an old slut, dumb,
She'll raise her skirts
For your quick look, but
It's the same ogle, buddy,
Want something wild? Want
Something crazy? Something . . . ?

Ah, she goes through the motions,
The same old struts and bumps,
And it takes a jaded eye
To catch anything new. She's
Recalcitrant, puts out fake shy,
Then tells all to anybody.

You want to peek something novel,
Con her into a fresh attitude?
She's tired, yawns easy. You
Gonna pay through the nose
And the heart for a second ticket.

Love Song in Age

for Philip Larkin

Love better not want no reward,
Said the old pimp looking back,
No john ever knew what I know,
No working stiff nor any man Jack,

And take this from a taker
Who never gave it free before,
Life has a last card up his sleeve
When you fall down for your old whore.

Down Home Question

Been gone a long time fella
Half the way to hell

Can ya tell me if my honey
Still carry water from the well

And if she carries water
Is there anyone long with her

Is there someone with that water
Goin home with her

Cause if there is ol fella
Cause if there is oh

Well whittle me a sharp stick
And push it in the sand

Tell her it hurt me that hard
When I am long and gone

Save it up till I'm out of sight
Then tell her all at once

Whittle it up stab it in the sand
Tell her all at once

Say I went the way to hell but
I'm still in love with her

No better not tell her that no
Just say you can't recall

And that I passed you straight on by
No don't say a word

Then none can say you lied old man
None can say you lied

But tell me if my honey
Carry water from the well

Tell me if my honey
Haul that water from the well

Down Home Answer

See by your eyes mister
You have had no home some time

See by your eyes mister
You knew our Emma Jean

And if you be her darlin
I'd be for leavin town

For they found her floatin last year
Wearin her weddin gown

Now I am just an old man
Haveta pay no mind to me

But I wouldnt stay here long son
Even to go and see

Wave to me up the road a ways
She was my daughter see

Wave to me up the road son
She loved you more than me

But that girl was my daughter
And she was right by me

Now I got a lot of whittlin
To do before its dark

But I'll whittle you a heart shape
Out of the purest bark

And I'll lay it in her flowers
Lighter than any lark

She never held no grudges
And I'm not gonna start

You run off like her mama
So I'm not gonna start

But if you get to Natchez
Or even see the Nile

Think of here as home always
And remember her a while

Music

I

Whole notes and half notes, big and little birds
Make telephone wires a staff of melody.
Nearby, a full bush cackles at random.

What do I think? I think
The whole world musics this morning,
Ordered or zany, centered or wry,

And I think so long last night,
Far away tomorrow. Day is
Sky enough to hold the huge singing.

II

Your fingers go here on the flute.
The thumb goes there. Now get
That's right only the other
Thumb rests here with nothing to do.

If song were simple, I could
Get the grip, I could wrap
My hands any way round the breath.

But my fingers go here on the flute,
The typewriter, the gun. Practice
Makes imperfect, too. You can hear
The valves of the heart miss a stop.

Choochoo Train

How we
Oh how we
Oh woe how we
Woe how we
Howhow howhow

Oh woe how we
Whowho
Oh woe

Loving Memory

I see it white tonight. I see Robert
At his door. I see the yellow flames
Of the tall candles burning halos
In the frosted windows. Robert Tucker,
Teacher at the door, you are New
England, all welcome from the cold.

Comic Poem

The G-men were ready
They knew that the crooks would
Snap at the bait

Hello Santucci
What can I do for you

Canayou use a some stuff

You are under arrest Santucci
I am a G-man

Ha ha onayou
I am a the C I A

Said the poet to his moll
Giggles

Sleight Of

Hey, here is the
Black silk top hat and
My hand reaches
Deep and by the long long ears pulls out

The white rabbit
You knew would happen out of force
Of habit.

But you fellow, readily deluded,
Wonder at this:

There is no rabbit no
Black silk ha ha top hat
And you and I are left with only these
Rapidly evaporating magic
Words.

Personal Effects
(1998)

Ada

When the good Contessa, her father's daughter,
Imagined she saw the music of the spheres
Strewn in the woven hair of the heavens,
Gossamer star notes of mathematic creation,
Her mind tasted the universe first hand, felt all,
Knew all, thought the great wordless poem of night,
Luminous dusts of golds and silvers in blowing tresses.

Her hands became combs of grace in the air thereafter.

The bones of her body were like bird bones then, like
Ballet bones, like flying dancers. Round and round
The constellations counted their journeys like stories
Written in light spans, poems alive in shining alphabets
Sprinkled like calculus visible as meteors waltzing.

No wonder she crazy gave half her father Byron's inheritance
To Invention. That huge wind within blew and clouds of
Number wove new thought paths and she could see
The measured midnight ballroom of the galaxies turning.

Her pale feet became lighter than any lover's ever after.

This night I take her tally card and sign my name.
I am her unknown suitor one hundred years too late,
But just in time. I ask her ladyship a whirl, a slight
Intoxication of the night. We sip and step
And then are double lost as dawn brings on its simple sight.

Ada, child, we are made of stars. Else how could I,
So far way, have seen them in your eyes? Men,
Some day, will send their ships to them. There
May be other life. There will be other poems. And we
Will weave our way through all of them. Your father
Must be proud of you. In me, is there a little of him?

Miami Heart

for Al Goldfine

Al is broke. He's flat on his back,
Needs triple bypass bad as I-95.
Them North Philly corpuscles,
Red in the face angry tail-lights,
Can't get where they want to go.
Life blood can't get to the beach.

The other drivers yawn, light up, while over
Caribbean airwaves the Latin beat goes on.

Dr. Blankstein looks up Al's vein with a glass eye,
Spots the tie-up. This guy, this pal, this hubbie,
This lover needs a lift, has to leave the fast lane.
Pull over, stop, says the good cop.
Stop, he detours the family. The red engine
Must idle. All close must idle.

No Will holds up in this court.
Technicians will try but, God's Will be done.
Only Jehovah and the priests of the pulse
Have a light enough touch. Who else
Cares so little so much? And Al, the good driver,
Must rumble and grumble, stuck in the flow
Between go and no go, oh,
Traffic engineers in white coats, wild
Vehicles with alarms and sirens, cut through,
Pass by, transcend all laws, speed him
To the Institute of the Heart.

Circled by masks like a stagecoach, Al is held up.
They pry his treasure chest, finger his value.
Goldfine, Goldfine, fat of the land,
The walls of your wallet are triple A.
They pick your pockets, bow and allow
The medicared for to motor through.
We will return to shallow breathing.
Forget our own pumps once again.

So toss that warning ticket, Al,
Resume God speed. Add this
To the driving lessons
With those old heart throbs
Far back in tales of Philly,
On Turnpike yesterdays.

Tosa Mitsusada

at the Morikami Museum

Foot, beak, and feather make his art.
The white cranes glide and soar
And light to leap and flap.

He is as his nearby peach to the sun,
A mild imitator, but in mind
Red as a crane's headdress.

So they all fall pure as water
And rest and pose and preen.
Crane and pine grip the craggy shore.

Ink and colors on paper cascade.
Here is Tosa Mitsusada, Director.
There is no more Office of Painting.

Dry Tears

Lost long letters, never
Written, spoken only
Ever in slumber,
Answer to woman
Or some other writer,

Sleep crafted,
Deep dream drafted,
Not pen sent,
Not type faced.
Pent.
Not even hint worded.

A film reversed, syllables rumble
Slowly as boulders trucked
Up in cement to the huge
Dam. Waiting to burst,
It sits in the sun.

Begun, day life lips on.
Conversations end.
Recognitions dim.
Her. Him.

Dry tears. Soft warm loam.
Lost long poem.

Reader

He held the poem to his ear
As if to hear
Within those small black folds
The shores of other centuries,
The darting birds
Of someone else's beach,
The frothing surf, the lovers on a sheet,
And if he listened carefully enough
Amid the evershifting shells,
Across the perfumed air,
The tink of a blue bottle
With the corked whisper,
"Are you there?"

Country Poem

Poem from the farm should show some hokum,
Touch of a fly leg quiver the flank
Squeeze such a poem and hot raw milk,
Straight from the teat, squirts in the eye.
Big hired hands may slap their knees, but
Poems from the country long to be courted,
Asked to the dance one month in advance.

Then the fiddle will diddle and the step be spry,
Old folk rocking round all around
And the kids'll peek from the loft in the sky
While the rafters lift with laughter swelling,
So later oh later when the stove is red
And girl dreams tumble in the goose down bed,

Toes will curl from the telling.

Art in Heaven

to W. B. Yeats

I mean to go. Your brochure
Tops the rest, and I see sails every day,
Yours in my dreams. But Byzantium,
So far away, even by jet,
And I can't spare the time this year.

The sages sound great, but T. S.,
Who knows about culture, says
One can't always expect them to give audience.
From what I hear, some siren
Would probably grab me, or
The way things are on my travels,
I would most likely fall into the sea.
The wings are always the first to go.

I get caught up, of course,
In such visions of Greek island vacation,
White temples atop rock, all else sun blue,
No one hum drum. You
Won't give up, I know, till I am there.
Think how much we will have to share.

Whiteout

There is an eighth day of the week,
Sitting in the calendar like a pocket
Door, a divider. Think it the
Hidden day of a personal leap year.

In your own house, in your own dark,
It is a door you might meet face flush.
It would explain the meaning of night.
This would happen only when you
Were familiar with the surroundings,
One might say completely absorbed.

You will not find the eighth day
Printed like a notable birth day.
This day of your death exists
In the whiteness of calendars.
It stretches on like the Arctic.

And I am told by men whose bones
Have learned how thick and deep
Cold flake can fall, too much
Looking for it makes you blind.

Cat Sonnet

A brown shopping bag borrowed from mother,
A collection of grass snakes
Gripped by twist handles, then dumped directly,
After calling Sylvester, on the sundial center
Of the great green lawn bounded by hedges.

First an untangle. And then, like degrees
Defining a circle, they hissed to circumference,
One paw on a tail, one paw on a tail, till
Mad cat sat exhausted, boy was befuddled, all got away.

Lost poems, I would say to that cat now, lost loves.
But none of our surviving lives knew, together,
The power of noon overhead in the summer,
How quick fear can rush us, how novelty fades,
How delicate life, and how slithery days.

Occupational Hazards

Trouble is, I wish each shrink a poet,
Each pol, each priest, each engineer.
Gaze at the Brooklyn Bridge, or fat Buddha.
Look at Mao. Listen to the struggles of Sigmund,
Sit in the radium room with the burns of Pierre.

As poet, you can say I'm expert
At aspiration, a kind of pro at hope.

Most call the hand of the dealer too soon.
This ain't black jack. If chains
Go with the office, think thrice about
Your dreams as a novice, what
You wanted the world to be, when it grew up.

Melville

When you pried noon from the blue
Where God had nailed it,
And rang it down on the equator,
Doubloon for Ahab,

                a great stab
Went through me on my coffin couch
And I rose up with blooded brow.

I am afraid that I am Ishmael now.

Eucharist

to G. M. Hopkins

I am sure those near heard your pen shriek,
All that woe from the black ink well.
Jesus. Each joy of the earth
Gold as a Christmas toy. Faith
For the falcon's life. Despair
On the nun's death. Every thing
Spur for a passion without tether,
Each Easter sheet a wafer without measure.

Two Sides

"*Sa mère*," her family called the old lady.
My mother would sigh at the inlaws implying
Each brother was trying to fob his origin
Off on the other. *Sa mère*.

"His mother" rocked in the house of her daughter,
Crocheting away in the great bay window
One doily a day to be wafted away for
The overstuffed sofas and divans that
Crowded the family parlors. How French.
How Canadien. Oh Quebec! Ah Mont Royale!

And I would watch from the rug on
Occasional visits, the little lady in
Black with white lace, silver needles
Hooking white thread with incredible
Speed. Click click, quick quick,
Delicate as her goodbye hand in my hair.

My mother's mother, now, warm as a great hen,
Would open her huge arms like an oven
To any child, dog, cat, and once even
I remember a torn sparrow flutter in her
Palm. She lived in Ludlow, up three flights
Over the grocer, and she snuck me nickels
For licorice when no one was looking.

I remember "It's all right, it's all right."
And "It doesn't matter, it doesn't matter."
And after her broken hip on the icy stair,
I see her in Florida surrounded by daughters,
Dark Ruth, blonde Janice, redhead Lolita.
And she would recall son George dead in the war.

Mothers and mothers of mothers and mothers
Of fathers, think and think again on
All your dear sons and dear daughters
Before we are scattered to town and to time
And lost to both living and dying,
Sa mère, ma mère, grand-mère Carrie.

Two en Route

Flat Out
Full throttle, high beam,
Fuel low, mix lean,
Gear up, nose down,
No airstrip to be seen.

Anchorage
I flew to the face of Mount
McKinley, slowed and hung.
I like my poem like that.
Sipped oxygen to burn the lung.

Two from Home

Dear Cat,

Like you, I want to be taken
And by the nape of my neck shaken,
I want some poem to pet me,
Overwhelming love reach down and get me.

August Harvest

Pluck them down quick, love,
Even down green,
Before the black bird come
To pick the tree clean.

Business Plan

I

It looks like fair weather, Icarus said
To press and to crowd, and please note the lead
In the shoes keep the feet safely under the head.
The glue on each quill is straight from Greek bees
And not one of these feathers is from overseas.
I will be covered by glamour and glory—
They will all want a pair when they hear my story.

II

... then Daedulus, with a new wax,
Plus scientific review of the facts,
Said to investors, I have a ton
More good ideas, and one younger son.
Your ducats are safe, the projections are sound,
And we'll lower the risk in the next public round.

To Walk Thin Ice

One simply need
Let go the land,
The planned.

Set out light.
Have no fear.
Leave everyone who has been near.

Leave well enough alone.
Feel self edge out on its own.

Cruises

Having little imagination,
They decided to travel,
Not finding the strange
In any of their friends.

They have gathered here from Duluth,
Lake Oswego, Sacramento,
And already they are busy
Examining gaily dressed neighbors
For superficial resemblance
To relatives.

They will complain in San Juan
About the age of the taxi,
The hike up to the rain forest,
And when they at last
Find the American island,
It will not be
American, completely,
Or enough.

And making for home,
The leg will be long,
And the long dinners
Will lengthen like the nights,
And exactly as they did
On the way out,
They will tell each other stories
About who stayed at home,
And the couple on the last cruise,
Who were scandalous.
And kept to themselves.

Choice

Ocean blue and forest green, I heft you in each
Hand, a kind of balance. The spines are bowed
From, over the years, my repeated reach.

Frost on the one hand, Yeats on the other,
I felt like the Pequod, heavy with fish,
Or the boy in the play between father and mother.

Now lost with the lost and with no way to go
The world is all woods and the world is all sea
And there are no directions for people like me.

Shakespeare

Fourteen terms I thumbed those rounded plays
With students, starting from the early days
Of mixed-up laughter, error and disguise
Then the whole History of English lies.
I did Hamlet by candle, choked Desdemona dead,
Macbethed until they said the walls went red,
A wise-mad raving with the fool-king Lear
Ended the year.
                Don't call again. Hack
Your own book from your own bloody back.
I have retired too prosperous to grieve
On the last tempest up his seamy sleeve.

Knockout

Anyone can get caught. A left hook
Flush on the cheek puts any good man down.
So you trained, ate right, ran
Morning miles around the entire town.

Did you think you were alone? Off
In another city, another rose with the sun
And struggled through his skipping day.
You met. And you were even. Till he won.

Old Twist

The great square knot of my body is ill
At ease. It wants to unravel its
Puzzle, perhaps? Take arms.
So much like legs, they have turned
The world upside down, for love
Or money. I often complain
I dangle from my own rigging.
And have been called some fumbler.

But I shall take the thumb of my left hand
And the big toe of my right foot,
As if they were the first and last
Words of a verse, and slyly work
Them together till the braid opens.
You can see I am at the ends of my rope.

Exercise #1

Sit still. Now turn your head
Far right. Look straight behind you.
Do the same to the left.

I have struggled with this
For a year. If you succeed,
You will view your own wake.

Which will serve well on a ship
Of fools. Even docked,
You may discover uses, perhaps political.

Don't say I didn't try to help.

Playthings in the Playhouse

"The playthings in the playhouse of the children.
Weep for what little things could make them glad."
—from "Directive" by Robert Frost

The day that game and all games fell away,
Nine apes danced upon the summer lawn.
No one kept score, nor
Remembers who played what. All, all
Was lost.

I hung my glove and put away my ball.
It always had been someone else's bat.
I took positions that I had to learn
By playing. Now
I had found everything at last.

The headlong dash for first,
The midfield social blur,
Third on a sacrifice,
Each runner runs away from home
To make it safe to home.

I followed your directive, coach of coaches,
Found the forgotten farm, the hidden cup,
And my own spring. God bless Saint Mark.

To read a word you must already
Know the word. The line
To know the line. The life
Must learn itself by reading backward
Silently, and to itself.

O Ludlow, O great green Massachusetts place,
New English streams and lanes
Of so much leaf the sky is green,
O memory of strength and youth
And play, and play, and play.

Once a professor asked,
"What is the meaning of your poem?"

You, half sad, all serious,
"Don't you know?"

O Robert Frost, and Yeats, Keats, William S.,
And you, shy Caedmon, come.
Drink and dance again for me the short, short while.

The Laureate Game

for Philip Larkin

You won our Eliot? We took
Your Auden. Losing a queen,
We are reduced to double rook.
Both know bishops are slant,
Hierarchies mean.
Each shore can hear each other's cant.

Crusades show knights straight forward, but
Having an angle. Every king and crook
Resigns the field rather than yield.
Why are you more ours than Theodore,
The Great?

The answer jumps out black and red:
No move you make is traditionally dead.
I am American. Check,
Mate.

Alaska Tandem
for William Stafford

I write you. You write me.
A pair of air mail poets
In transcontinental talk.

Your letter remembers that split
Second the shutter caught
You casual, against my prop.

Oh that day the drop, banking the valley,
Running rail road track,
Wing tip beneath spruce top,

With neither a shout nor a shock
At that grand illusion of speed whirled
In flight so tight to the world.

Remembering My Liberal Education
a dedication

I had to look up in Webster's Universal the word *Liberal,* meaning
"Generous, free, not small minded, not bigoted."

I had to look up the word *Educate,* from the Latin, meaning
"To lead forth from wrongness and ignorance."

I had to look up the word *Art,* meaning
"The making and doing of things which have form and beauty."

Busy life has filled my heart and head. Old now,
I must sit down in this place of public wealth, this place
We have given one another, and study with you quietly
And without haste, how we might live more free,
Ignore truth less, learn how we might form and make
Beauty for each other and for our children
As others throughout history labored to educate us.

Regret Park

Deep in the thicket green,
I shot. A spot
Of yellow fell. It

Has fallen fifty years
To these feet,
Sitting here.

Tiny, bloody eye,
To see so far
You cloud my sky.

Cultures

Look, the Present is expanding at the speed
Of fright. There is more news now
Than all history, milling crowds
Of inglorious Miltons, mobs
Of Napoleons, more jets than, say,
Pterodactyls. One can be snatched
Up and off, like Sinbad, to Sumatra.

I am writing this in one language
Of many languages, trying to raise,
Like Lazarus, my voice from the dead.
Look, this is not an antique design.
These are not hieroglyphics. I
Have left my face behind me. Listen,
Listen to me. I want you to know my tongue.

The Poem in America

Tough go up North. Magazines want
Travel poems to sell tour ads. Book
Publishers won't give collections a look.
Friends of the board win the prize, get the grant,

While Ecuadorian bartender Ray,
Alive with the poets of Quito, can say
His relatives sing, and his sister makes plain
The tastes of the air in a mountain refrain.

Fruits

The Home called. His ashes were ready.
My wife picked them up, brought them to mother.
The two stepped into the Florida dusk,
Young woman helping old woman, and
Under the darkening grapefruit tree
He was so proud of he reclined
Hours days weeks watching it
Blow lemon bubbles, mother softed his ashes.
Then they returned to the light. Finally,
She washed her tired hands of him.

In Age

Tell me when it went wrong, body, say
What snake frightened the horse high.
I. The I that began sentences strong,
Rhymed loud in the quiet night, sang
The day long, measured, composed,
Arranged, noted this morning the dawn
Pale fingered. Was there a flaw
Even before the departure? Ignored
Under the hubbub of beginning? Over

Looked? Done then, eh? Grown the play
To such major proportions it must end
Untidy, in mild audience dismay? Ah, men.
One leg up, all seemed propitious. Then.

Late Night

We wanted the afternoon cartoon,
The Saturday cowboy. We would boo
The travelog of strange downtowns,
Peasants in the paddies in the fields,
We wanted Hopalong and Mister Magoo,
How to get the girl in the saloon.

Where did all the audience go?
They left on their lives, though
I am still in the dim half dark,
Gripping my popcorn and my coke,
Watching projected pictures of Chinese
Put into space and bounced back to my eyes.
This year's dialog is how much rice.

I got some girls from some saloons,
Outwitted here and there a crook,
Though now I have a billion yellow friends,
I sit unsure how world should work,
Even how anybody's story ends.

I have been careful with my bricks and straw
And wear the badge of my small town.
Why do I feel some uninvited wolf
Is drawing his deep stratospheric breath
To blow mine and all our houses down?

Ideally

I love you so much
My ribs can't hold up
The skin of my legs
Anymore, writes K. P.

That's
Poetry. That's
Presumption. That's
What we all want to hear.

We readers are greedy.
We fuss and we fizz.
We want the love poem
To be about us.

But maybe we're needy.
And maybe it is.

Giverny

The bright green pads oval deep green shadows
On the long pond's mottled floor, a shallows-
Woven canvas: fog whited, dawn tinted,
The scent of silent lucent water hinted.

Sun upon sun, an evergilding sun,
Interrupting clouds, dim darks of rain,
The subtle pallet moon, dark darks of night,
Transform each leaf and bloom with prism light.

A garden castle with a willow moat,
A lilyflower lady in a boat,
A fading pigment permanence of mists,
All floating constellate. Like morning myths.

Open, Lily, for this poem I pray,
For waking Paris needs you. And Monet.

Duet

Death?
                        Sir.

If?
                        None.

Until?
                        Gone.

When?
                        Over.

Remembrances of Things Past

Jaw slack, I let my tongue relax,
Protrude through the teeth
Like a cat. Like the
Cat on my lap, purring.

I purr in sympathy, two purrers.
Slowly my tongue swells, the Old Mind
Before Teeth hums. Lips puff.
All is taste. I should have known that.

A poem turns on meditation.
It should pull its tail in, like
The cat is now doing. Who said,
All things come around? Basho,
Watching his Japan cat in that
Hut. No, in front of the hut.
And both sitting. And in the sun.

St. Paul's Church
to John Donne

I paid the pence and
Ran around the altar,
Stopped, and stood.

There you were,
John, in your
Hood.

Dedication

for the Gregory Wolfe Student Center

The place, he said once, survives the man. As if
He knew. As if any place could be the same after
Gregory. Named for a Saint, what faith
He shows that Man can understand the foreign, even
In himself. Today we dedicate a place of youth
To a man who studied men, a place in our hearts
To a man young with our perennial praise,
A place to exemplify an international president
Who lives like Art: Soul centered, forever resident.

White on White

Are you numb?
Asks Doctor Jerry. Bite
Down, back and forth some.

He needs a good impression
Of my upper reaches. Oh,
Jerry, so do I.

Then I am let go
And leave, stretch, sigh,
Look to the sky.

None too soon.
A great flight of white pelican
Just bit the morning moon.

Aft to Bridge

No QE2 will see our likes again.
Thirty years might be once more re-engineered,
But no new stabilizers will even our keels,
Then deeper in darker waters, more dread
Than this light North Atlantic squall
As perfect harp cello flute play
Joplin for the sandwiches and tea.

Ah, me. Read this flung over the side to bob
And bob to your sun bathing on some shadowless isle.
Ba sik, a Viking would axe in rock, *bathe your self.*
Tragedy passes. Hope, too. *Thisses swa maeg,
This also might.* We take the Concorde home.

Epilogue

Most poets end without the real work done. Most
Never thread the thought they thought when young.
That great poem one would weave later never ever
Satisfied the bright anticipator. Oh, when much
Was hoped and some begun, the least was most
We truly won. I know this because I spun
So many skeins and cards and weaves that I
Am old as fabric is to the pull of wool. All said
And done, the best is lost. Old poets weep as one.